THE STORY KEEPER :
A MEMOIR OF
LOVE AND SURVIVAL

WORKBOOK PRESS
RECOMMENDED
LITERARY BOOK COMPETITION

ERNARD A. PENDRY

WORKBOOK PRESS LLC
187 E Warm Springs Rd,
Suite B285, Las Vegas, NV 89119, USA

Website: https://workbookpress.com/
Hotline: 1-888-818-4856
Email: admin@workbookpress.com

Ordering Information:
Quantity sales. Special discounts are available on quantity purchases by corporations, associations, and others.
For details, contact the publisher at the address above.

Library of Congress Control Number:
ISBN-13:   978-1-955459-49-5 (Paperback Version)
               978-1-955459-50-1 (Digital Version)

REV. DATE: 21/05/2021

THE STORY KEEPER: A MEMOIR OF LOVE AND SURVIVAL

An Observation of Life

By Bernard A. Pendry

INTRODUCTION

Dear reader, whoever you are, I have indulged myself setting down various facets of my life, no mysteries or suspense just things that maybe of interest.

It has been, and still is, a wonderful life, many ups and only a few downs. From the index you will get an idea of what is included.

I make no apologies for mistakes because memories fade but with the help of my diaries from 1948 onwards I hope there are not too many.

Cheers

Must give a special thanks to my wonderful wife, Sue, who has helped me every step of the way and has edited every word. So if you find any errors blame her not me.

BOOK REVIEW FOR MR. PENDRY'S MEMOIR

The author of this book immediately gripped my attention and sparked my imagination as he took my hand and led me in through a time-tunnel, stepping out at the other end into a whole other world full of fun and shocking adventures. Sound familiar? - it's not. It is so much deeper than that.

Upon reading, many a time my heart sank with raw sadness. I experienced fears of things alien to me since the Pendry family keeps on moving and moving the end of the war times. And yet, my perception of control and of time began to morph as I found myself intrigued by new concepts, wanting to soak it all in, absorbing not just the thrills and adventures but also this whole new way of both thinking and surviving.

Bernard highlights not that anything is just simply possible or achievable, but demonstrates how to make it so, should you so choose. This is something that ordinarily does not come easy, is outside of one's comfort zone and, in these global times in which I write this review, reaches, and inspires me on a level that I had never believed possible. When the author's Dad even passed away, the Will was unbelievable because it left the latter with nothing.

As much as I loved the thrills, adventures, the highs, and the lows, the memoir filled me with wonder, opening both my mind and my imagination long after I'd finished reading the book. The concepts of Time, the interconnections between past, present, and future, the connections with history which, can also repeat itself. The ability to laugh in adversity and overcome life challenges, the qualities of each person and what made them and, the varying connections between people both present, and past.

To almost step inside the authors mind, and his world, has been a unique honor and experience, and one that acts as a tool in life should we be brave enough to dare ourselves away from the world as we know it, and embrace a refreshing, more truthful perception, leaning not on our false crutches, but by returning to the true wonders of our world in which we live.

I find the chapter's title very catchy and appropriate. I was also impressed on the timeline presented by the author, and was even hooked on the fact that his memoir goes beyond to what happened in their family, most especially with the main characters: Mum & Dad, brother Reg, Sheila (1st wife), Sue (my third wife) and others.

Now I can say that we need to focus on the right people who will be interested to buy a memoir and to appreciate the lesson and value of it beyond the story.

-Workbook Press Book Reviewer-

INDEX OF CHAPTERS

INDEX OF APPENDECES

MY WHITE SUIT

Bernard Pendry

CHAPTER 1

THE EARLY LIFE &
TIMES OF MUM & DAD

Dad was born in February 1903 to a world in change, the first Electric Tram in Clapham, The Ford Motor Company formed, The Wright Brothers got into the air with their FLYER all of 850 feet and Queen Victoria had died in 1901 so King Edward 7th was on the throne.

I know nothing of Dad's early life except for a school class photo at age 9. There were 35 boys in the class, only one wearing glasses all dressed in wide, stiff, white collars, ties and dark blazers.

Before Mum was born in 1908 there had been historic events,

Rolls & Royce had teamed up to launch a business,

First electric tube train on the Metropolitan Line from Baker Street to Uxbridge,

San Francisco had a devastating earthquake,

Auguste & Louis Lumiere discovered how to make moving pictures,

Baden-Powell forms the Boy Scouts movement,

Old Age Pension introduced at 5 shillings (25p) per week,

First London Olympic games at White City Stadium, 1500m record 4.03,

Jack Johnson becomes the first black world heavy weight champion.

The start of the Edwardian period.

Mum was born on 29th November 1908 to Hannah May Green at Ely Street, a rundown part of Fulham just off the North End Road, which you would now call a slum. Their second floor flat was only two rooms, with no inside running water, no electricity and a toilet down stairs. On 11th February 1911, sister Kit was born. At this stage, Hannah was not married so it is impossible to know what sort of life she had led, and how she had born two children out of wedlock in an age where unmarried women were frowned upon. The girls went to school with surnames of Green. At some stage, she got together with David Peter Ruse, for some reason called Charlie, and they started producing children first being Bunny (after whom I'm christened) in 1914 and another 7 followed ending with Len in 1927. Can you imagine all these living in two rooms? Alice & Kit changed their name by deed poll to Ruse, unfortunately their Mum died at age 42 so they never got the chance to find out who their true father was.

Mum was an incredibly beautiful lady evidenced by a prized black and white photo of her taken when she was 17. I thought it must have been taken in a professional studio but she assured me it was just a snap by a friend. Her dark wispy hair, black eyes that stare straight at you, pert nose and perfect bow lips with the overall appearance of a Spanish gypsy girl. It sits in pride of place in my study.

Charlie was the stable master for the Express Dairy's horses in North End Road where there were rows of stables on either side with the name of each horse painted of the stable door. All the kids enjoyed visiting to marvel at how incredibly big all the horses seemed to be.

During all these years there had been major events:

    1909. Selfridges opens in Oxford Street the largest store in England

    Saucy postcards appear

    Louis Bleriot flies the Channel

    Pearl Harbour Naval Base is built to thwart

any Japanese invasion

1910. Thomas Alva Edison discovers how to combine pictures and sound.

Captain Roger Falcon Scott and party die trying to reach the South Pole. Roald Amundsen succeeded.

China annexed Tibet.

1911. Shop workers win right to a 60-hour week.

Record heat wave 97 degrees.

Woman's Weekly launched.

1912. Titanic, the unsinkable liner hits an iceberg and sinks.

National Insurance Act.

1913. Suffragette Emily Davidson dies when jumping in front of the Queen's horse at the Epsom Derby

The Panama Canal opened by President Wilson.

1914. 28th June, Archduke Franz Ferdinand assassinated in Sarajevo, Bosnia. This sparks off the GREAT WAR and Britain declared war on Germany when they invaded Belgium. There followed nearly 4 years of a horrific war notably the trench battles of Ypres and the Somme. USA did not join the war until April 1917. Germany finally surrendered on 11th November 1918.

When war broke out Mum was 6 and Dad 11.

Other events:

1915. Women urged to work in factories.

1916. Subscription brought in. Dad missed it by a few years.

British Summer Time introduced.

1917.   First bombing of London.

1918.   School leaving age raised to 14.

The Russian Tsar and his family massacred after spending almost a year in Siberia.

Spanish Flu, thought to have started in either China or India accounted for 40 million deaths worldwide.

Women over 30 may now vote.

1919. Prof. Rutherford splits the ATOM

First air service London to Paris 3 hours 30 minutes.

Alcock & Brown fly the Atlantic in 16 hours 12 minutes.

1920.   Prohibition in the USA.

Bloody Sunday. IRA kills 14 soldiers.

1921.   Women allowed to sit on juries for divorce cases.

Ireland given independence

1922.   The Jazz Age in full swing in the USA.

Tutankhamun's tomb unearthed by Howard Carter's team

First regular NEWS broadcast.

1923.   New Divorce Bill. Equal rights for women.

German Marks basically worthless, a barrow load for a loaf of bread.

Hitler's Brown Shirts forms the Nazi party.

Bernard Pendry

In 1923, Mum, trailed by some of her siblings, went for the weekly shopping to North End Road street market with stalls of every description on both sides. Eldest sibling Bunny ran ahead, and when she caught up, he was chatting to a handsome looking man, both of them wearing a Fulham Football t-shirt. The conversation went, "Sorry, I hope he is not bothering you." The gentleman replied, "Not at all. We were just discussing this afternoon's game. Will you be going?" "I sometimes go but not this week, too much to do" by this time Bunny had lost interest and wandered off. "By the way, my name is Jim, and both my friend and I are season ticket holders, he cannot come to next week's game so would you like to accompany me?" "I'm Alice, and yes, I would love to come but I must dash off now as my tribe may be getting into trouble." "OK Alice be on the corner of Langthorn Street opposite the turnstiles at 12.30 and I will be waiting." It was clear the way Alice skipped along smiling that she fancied Jim likewise he was smitten and couldn't wait for next Saturday. This was the start of their courtship.

I was in awe listening to Mum and Dad talk about their courtship days in the twenties. Life seemed untroubled, and their Saturday nights, before TV and radio distractions, seemed fun. They would go out to a pub with friends, Reg Swift, Bert Austin and others, and then back to someone's house who had a piano and spend hours singing all the popular songs that Dad never forgot and would continue to sing for the rest of his life. His trademark songs included 'Burlington Bertie', 'Let's Have a Little Bit More', 'Two Lovely Black Eyes' and many more. Once up, it was difficult (if not impossible) to get him down!

1924. First Winter Olympics in Chamonix. 18 nations took part.

Winston Churchill back in power. Back on the Gold Standard

1925. Cyprus becomes a British colony

Hitler's book Mein Kampf is published.

The Charleston craze in full swing.

Mum & Dad marry and the photos show the type of dresses for both young and old. I don't know if they honeymooned but she was pleased to be out of Ely Street and move in with her in-laws, although this didn't go too well as she found her mother-in-law very bossy. However this is where daughter Glad was born 1928.

This ended life as a couple, now family life.

The rest of the family stayed in Ely Street until 1943 when father Charlie died. This was apart from Bunny and Kit who had joined the forces.

MUM AT 18

THEIR WEDDING

DAD'S PARENTS

WEDDING GROUP

YOUNG DAD

GRAN & GLAD

MUM IN CARE HOME

MUM AT 99 WITH HER TWO BOYS

Bernard Pendry

CHAPTER 2

FAMILY LIFE OF MUM & DAD

They were thankful of moving from Eardley Crescent to a flat in Langthorn Street, Fulham near the Fulham Football Club where son Reg was born and a lasting friendship was made with Hetty & Sid Davey. Next move was to a flat in Atlanta Street where I was born in 1936.

In 1934, Dad had bought a beach hut in Whitstable, Kent in the Thames Estuary, the equivalent to a millionaire buying a villa on The Costa del Sol. What a wonderful place for holidays and weekend breaks. It was dark green with a few steps leading to a veranda before entering a very cozy room. There was a bench seat along the right side, cupboards at the back, occasional chairs, an old fashion tall gas heater and a primus stove that needed pumping to get it working.

It was in the middle of about 40 beach huts right in front of the toilet and washhouse blocks. To get to it, once off the tarmac road, it was along a gravel track with the Whitstable Golf Club on one side just behind the main line railway line and the beach on the other. The 'beach' was not like the golden sands of the Costa, total pebbles until the tide went out, then it was the Thames Estuary mud, ideal for cockling.

I have many photos of me as a toddler with Dad, Glad and Reg frolicking in the sea, and photos of the friends who stayed with us. Dad's swimming costume was certainly risqué, a full length knitted affair, which was respectable when dry, but sagged horribly when wet. These were the happiest days of Mum's life, enjoying a relaxed time with family and friends, and joining in evening COCKELING when the tide went out. We would walk past the shingle, then on to mud (some would call it sand), hunting for cockles. There are various signs where a cockle may be, look for a small circle, a little darker than the surround, or look for two 'eyes' poking up, then insert a finger deep down and hope to bring up a cockle. Having finished this hunting, Mum would put our haul into a bucket filled with heavily salted water. They would be left overnight to spit out whatever sand they may have, then into boiling water (what a way to go). Delicious with a piece of bread!

The main railway line ran along the back of the beach huts, and at the far end, there was an unmanned level crossing over which a lane leads up to the town with a wall on the right. It was thrilling, standing just over the crossing, leaning against the wall listening to the rumble of a train coming down the line, getting louder and louder, your heart pumping then bursting past, just feet away.

This idyllic situation was shattered by the Second World War when the government decreed that all beach huts had to be removed or blown up to stop Jerry using them as cover should they invade. However, in 1949, with the war finally over, another beach hut was purchased DIY style. It was loaded onto a hired lorry and Dad, 'uncle' Bert, Reg and I set off to erect it on the same spot as the old one. The lorry was driven along a gravel track to the very spot, hut unloaded, then Bert decided rather than back along the track, he could do a quick turn around on the beach. Off he went down the shingle but as soon as he turned, big wheel spin. Dad rounded up a group of holidaymakers and with some effort, got it back on track. We continued using it for many years but as us, kids, found other things to do so it was sold. Still wanting a bolthole, they bought a caravan in Munday's Holiday camp near Bognor.

Years later, Reg and I visited the area where our hut had been. It seemed so down market with not a lot going for it. Don't get this confused with Whitstable town, which is a romantic place to visit.

THEIR FINAL MOVE

In 1941, Dad bought the freehold of 42 Ringmer Avenue, Fulham, which would be the family home until we boys married in 1959, and where they would spend the next 40 years. It is a 4-bedroom terraced house, Mum & Dad had the big first floor front bedroom, Reg the middle, and mine at the back overlooking the garden, well a yard 12 square feet that Dad paved with the cheapest oddment of slab stones possible.

There was also a 'cellar' commonly known as a 'coal cellar' where regularly the coalman, wearing a traditional leather hat with protection down his back, shot bags of coal down the small coalhole just outside the front door. You hoped it was genuine anthracite but often there was slag, which didn't burn well, and spat sparks all over the place. The coalman had a mighty horse and cart, and if the horse decided to relieve itself, it was a race to fill your bucket with good manure for the garden. Not only was the cellar for coal, it was Dad's workshop and housed the gas meter that had to be fed regularly with ten-penny pieces to keep the gas flowing.

The door to the cellar didn't shut properly, and in the evening, it was dark, foreboding and sinister. I had to pass this on the way to bed, fearsome that some monster would leap out, so I would whistle and sing before making a dash. Well, I am still here to tell the tale.

Downstairs was a 'front room' only ever used on special occasions like when aunts & uncles visited, so the three-piece sofa was as good as new years later, a scullery (now you would call it a kitchen) which really was Mum's work room, cooking, and a big boiler for washing where the weeks washing would be put in on a Sunday night for a soak, ready for the Monday wash. I have fond memories of the mangle that Mum encouraged us to put through as much washing as we could manage (no such thing as electric dryers). At the rear was the dining/living room where we ate, played records, darts and cards, especially crib that Dad and I played endlessly. Mum also used to cover the dining table and use it as her ironing board.   It opened onto the back yard where during the war, an Anderson shelter was installed.

 (In 2017, son Mark going past the property noticed it was up for sale, so Sue and I arranged a visit. True, they had done a lot of work on it, rooms in the loft, cellar livable but nowhere did I think it merited the asking price of £1.9 million). I wonder what Dad paid for it!

REG

My brother, Reg was born in 1930 and as he was 6 years older than me, we had little in common in the early years but I do remember one rather special occasion. Mum & Dad were going to a Ladies Night, and for the only time I can remember, instructed Reg to stay home and look after his 12 years old brother. This was a Saturday night, so no way was he going to stay in "Bernard, get your coat on. We are going out", and off we went to The Hammersmith Palais. What an experience. I was still in shorts, and Reg must have been a regular as a quick chat to the doormen and in we went to be met by a bevy of young ladies who made a real fuss of me. The light shining on the glitter ball, the music of the resident band, the dancers were just magical.

Read about his absconding in The War Years.

When he left school, he did get a job in a draughtsman's office, soon realizing he did not like working in an office, so followed in Dad's footsteps and became an electrician. Years later, after Dad had retired, they went into business as Ionic Electric, renting a property right opposite the Fulham Library.

He did cause Mum and Dad some concerns when he got in with the wrong crowd at Walham Green (changed to Fulham Broadway in 1952). Nothing serious but the local newspaper had a down on them. He joined the Navy in 1948 patrolling the North Sea in HMS Truelove, did get promoted to corporal (or the Navy equivalent), but was soon demoted for fighting while in Norway. A few of the sailors had gone into a dance hall in town, where a group of US soldiers had erected a large Stars and Stripes flag. Reg and his mates tore it down, and all hell let loose with everyone fighting. He told me that he was fighting a Yank outside and threw a punch as the Yank collapsed; his arm kept going and dislocated his shoulder. He brought home some interesting presents from his travels: sealskin slippers for Mum (that she claimed were uncomfortable), and a set of hunting knives for me, that I still have.

ENTERTAINMENT

Dad used to book tickets (well in advance) for front row seats, way up in the Gods at The London Palladium, where we saw such famous artists as Max Miller, Max Bygraves, Anne Shelton, Frankie Lane, Liberace and (an act I will always remember), Rudi Horn on his one wheeled bicycle throwing cups, saucers, spoons etc onto his head! One artiste who really surprised us was Johnny Ray, an American crooner who seemed to have hearing difficulties as he always held a hand over one ear! Dad thought he would just be a laugh, but he was fantastic.

Dad also got us in to watching Ice Hockey at Earls Court. Although Mum found it difficult to follow the puck, it was hilarious listening to her keep shouting *'where's the puck?' 'where's the puck?'*

Dad also arranged trips to London Olympia for wrestling. Our favourites (or villains according to your views) were Jackie Pallow, Mick McManus, Les Kellet, Tibor Szakacs and many others. These were fun outings enjoyed by us all. Unfortunately, in my opinion, British Wrestling was ruined when Big Daddy and Giant Haystacks came along. Just two big lumbering heavy weights, that won most bouts by smothering opponents with their large bellies. Soon after wrestling (as we knew it) was taken off the telly.

FULHAM FOOTBALL CLUB

Every week Dad and 'Uncle' Bert went to football, Fulham when they were at home and Chelsea when they were away (to cheer the opposition!).

I used to go with them and enjoyed the experience. However, getting out of the ground was an ordeal for youngsters, as going up the steps towards The Cottage (the building containing the director's box) it got narrower and narrower causing the crowd to get denser and denser. I still remember the relief as you passed the narrowest point to safety and home for Mum's delicious Welsh rarebit!

The players I remember from those days are Johnny Haynes, Len Quested, Chennell (the left back with an enormous chest), Joe Buccuzie who for a time lived in our road and with whom I played golf, Arthur Stevens a fast right winger who joined from the Arsenal but was afraid of a tackle and of course Jimmy Hill all action, little skill who later challenged the limiting wage structure and made Johnny Haynes the first £100 a week footballer also he was called in by the Football Association to see if he could suggest a way to make the points system more exciting. Since the start of the leagues 100 years ago it had always been two points for a win and one for a draw. It was he who came up with the current system, three points for a win. It made an incredible difference.

BOXING DAY TRIP TO TONBRIDGE

Another highlight of my parent's year was their Boxing Day trip to Sid and Aunt Davy's down at Tonbridge (friends from their time at Langthorn Street). I used to go until age 16 then it was more fun getting my mates (Archie, Doug, Fred, Mick and Ginge) round for a couple of days horse racing at Kempton Park, cards, drinks at the pub in Colehill Lane.

On one trip down there a rear tyre on Dad's Morris 8 went flat. For some reason he didn't have a jack so what could he do? Just then a couple of sturdy Canadian soldiers came along and lent a hand. They simply tipped the car over onto two wheels long enough for Dad to put on the spare tyre!

THE FREEMASONS

Dad had a number of passions (apart from Mum) not least of which was being a member of The Hemming Lodge based in Twickenham where he would attend Lodge of Instructions most Monday nights to help the newcomers and the monthly Lodge meetings. He could recite the words of every ritual eventually reached the rank of Grand Lodge Officer.

However, my own view of the Masons is not favorable. Although Dad never approached me directly, but knowing how he loved it, I thought I would have a go. So he was pleased to introduce me to his lodge. To become a full Mason you have to get through three initiation ceremonies (or "degrees" as they were called), all pretty easy, essentially just remembering a few lines. The third degree is the one where the right trouser leg is rolled up, you are blindfolded and, assuming your recital of the lines is successful, the blindfold is removed and you 'see the light'. It is then you can buy your apron and other regalia also be welcomed into lodges around the world.

From then on you are expected to attend Lodge of Instruction meetings to learn about the craft, and make gifts to charity. I attended one of these and declared it a waste of time. You were also expected to attend the monthly lodge meetings that start at 4 o'clock. These were no better.

I would leave my office (where I was very busy), to get to Twickenham before 4pm. just in time to get into the lodge before 'the outer guard' closed the door. I would then sit in the back row to watch the proceedings. There were a series of 'rituals' repeated parrot fashion as they had been done for centuries. It was difficult not to fall asleep, and indeed I often did.

Getting no enjoyment, I transferred to The Francis Drake Lodge in Sutton because a number of squash friends were members. Same result. So I threw in the towel and ended my association with the Masons. It remains a mystery to me why so many people enjoy being a Mason. I guess it's the appeal of 'belonging' to a group, or maybe a way of picking up business, or perhaps just getting away from 'her indoors!'

It was not for me.

THEIR DANCING.

Dad was a founder member of the Association of Supervising Electrical Engineers and every year he organized their Ladies Night dinner dances that Sheila (my 1st wife) and I got dragged along to. To watch Dad dance was fascinating: his right elbow kept going up and down as though he was trying to take flight, his feet shuffled in no particular order as he got hotter and hotter! I felt sorry for any lady he picked on.

Mum was not a dancer but I did give her a few lessons in our living room (the waltz being one) so he did get her onto the dance floor a few times. At one do he was in 'the Chair' and it was customary for the lady to be presented with a present. Most ladies had canteens of cutlery, cut glass vases, etc but not Mum… a new vacuum cleaner was wheeled in to the great mirth of all present!

VISITS TO THE OFFICE

Dad was very proud when I became a Chartered Accountant and later in life when I had my own office in the West End he would pop in for a chat and a cuppa sometimes served by Sue (who, some 38 years later became my 3rd wife!). To get there he would cycle his 'Golden' bike to the bus stop in Fulham Road, leave it there and catch the number 14 bus to Piccadilly. He was always made to feel most welcome, even though I could be involved in some important work.

THE GOLDEN BIKE

The Golden Bike is so-called because Reg and I presented it to him at their Golden Wedding party. Dad had given up cycling at that point, as he couldn't get his leg over! So Reg found this second hand ladies bike and had it sprayed gold. Dad thought it was terrific and rode it everywhere!

FLYING THE NEST

In 1959 both Reg and I left Ringmer as married men. Reg in February married to Sue (not my Sue), and me in May married to Sheila. However, we returned most Wednesday nights to play darts and cards. Mum would sit doing her crosswords and had many dictionaries, thesauruses, etc as aids. Sue started getting into crosswords and on one occasion asked for Mum's help. The clue was something to do with what a palm helmet was made of. Mum's answer was 'pith' to which Sue replied "I didn't know palms pithed" causing howls of laughter.

MUSIC AND FILMS

They had progressed from the wind up gramophone to a proper record player. Dad's favourites were Al Jolson, Flanagan and Allen, Gracie Fields, Anne Shelton, and Mum's were Howard Keel & Nelson Eddie.

Films of the day were movies such as 'The Third Man' with Orson Wells, 'The Blue Lamp' with Jack Warner, "Morning Departure" with John Mills (now Sir), and many others (those of you brave enough can trawl through my diaries to find out more!).

On the radio there was 'Take it from Here', 'Billy Cotton's Band Show', 'Educating Archie', and the like.

DAD'S CARS

His first car was a Morris 8 DLY448 and the leather upholstery made me feel sick so on any long journeys, like going to the beach hut, a pot was always on board. In1959 he really went up market and bought this magnificent black and cream, low-slung and sporty Sunbeam Rapier. Rather surprisingly, he let me use it for our second honeymoon in August 1959. Off Sheila and I set going north (I can't remember our destination) but on the first motor way in Britain (the Preston by pass), I reached the dizzy speed of nearly a100 m.p.h. No speed cameras in those days.

LIFE AFTER RETIREMENT

When Dad retired from mainstream employment in 1972, as I have said, he went into business with Reg as Ionic Electric. Apart from this he loved cycling his Golden Bike to the nearest 14 bus stop, which he didn't bother to lock up and board the bus up to Piccadilly or beyond and have a wander.

FAMILY MEET UPS

Most enjoyable occasions were the family garden parties I arranged at Ruxley Lane, where all the family (aunts, uncles, cousins and partners) were invited. Mum and Dad loved these as it meant they met up with family they hadn't seen in years and reminisced about all the years before.

DAD THE ROMANTIC

I never thought Dad was romantic, but after Mum died I found these incredibly romantic letters and cards that Dad had sent her when he was away on jobs. Just shows how little we know of those close to us.

GOLF & DIABETES

In his late 70s, Dad was diagnosed with diabetes but advised that if he adopted strict eating habits he would not need insulin injections. At this stage, he had packed up golf as he was overweight and getting frail but miraculously, because of these new eating habits (that included a pint or two of Guinness!), he lost weight and went back to playing golf!

DAD'S DEATH

My Dad died on 13th November 1984. The day before he died, he had cycled his Golden Bike round to the off license to buy his usual half bottle of whiskey for medical purposes. On his return he said *"Al, I don't think I can ride that bike any more."* That night he had a heart attack and died peacefully in bed.

I can't remember Dad having much stress in his life; he was a good man, got on with everyone and will be long remembered.

The reading of his will was a bit of a shock not only to me but also Mum. The house was left to Reg with Mum being able to live there for life I didn't even get a mention. Mum said she would have harsh words with him when they met! I did approach Reg and though he felt guilty said that is what Dad wanted. I can understand that Dad would have rationalized that I was doing OK financially but that is no excuse for not giving me a mention. It still hurts.

LIFE FOR MUM WITH DAD GONE

Mum carried on at Ringmer Avenue for a few years but had to move when Reg (the owner), got into financial difficulties and needed to sell Ringmer to release some funds.

These difficulties were caused by Reg borrowing substantial funds to renovate a property (1 Parsons Green) left to him and Sue by some old lady they had been looking after.

As Reg and Sue were now living in this property, they created a granny annex for Mum. However, she didn't particularly like living there, so Reg approached the council who found her a managed flat in Anselm Road (just off North End Road where Mum did all her shopping through the years). Very soon Reg got rid of 'Meals on Wheels' and cooked a meal for her every day.

When it wasn't safe for Mum to be on her own the council agreed to support a move to a care home, Grace Lodge, in Hinchley Wood (just down the A3). She thoroughly enjoyed the place, had her own room and downstairs had her own chair overlooking the beautiful gardens. Reg & I would visit her most Fridays and although there is little to discuss with an old lady in her 90's, we used to sing with her all the tunes from days gone by (I'll be with you in Apple Blossom Time', 'Underneath the Arches' etc).

Bernard Pendry

After a dodgy turn they decided she should move to a nursing home, so in 2005 (at the ripe old age of 98) she ended her days at Milverton Nursing Home another wonderful home where she passed away quietly in her sleep. You read much about nursing homes being criticised but my experience is they are fantastic

On one 1997 visit to Mum in Anselm Road there in an outside dustbin were many ancient photos of Mum & Dad's early years, their marriage, holidays at Whitstable etc. that I rescued. When asked why she had thrown them away she said "who on earth would be interested in photos that must be over 50 years old?" I assured her that not only me but also all the family would be keen to keep them.

Photos of Dad show him as a handsome man always smartly dressed with a mop of wavy hair.

On Mum's 90th birthday we had a family gathering outside the patio. The helpers were great and at one stage bought out a large tray of teas and cakes that were much appreciated. Being a good guest I decided to return the tray loaded with cups and saucers and set off only to find that my left leg wouldn't follow so it seemed like slow motion as I fell to the ground with an almighty crash. Those present thought I had had a seizure or something but what had happened was my trouser leg had got caught on the wheel of Mum's chair.

ME AS BABY   *DAD IN MASONIC REGALIER*

GOLDEN WEDDING

Bernard Pendry

CHAPTER 3

SCHOOL DAYS
&
EARLY SCHOOL LIFE

The first I remember is **Munster Road Infants School** and then the only recollection is me and my friend, Piggy Clark, going round the playground one behind the other going 'choo choo choo' pretending we were a train.

Next was **Sherbrook Road School**, now a block of flats. These should have been informative years building up to the 11 plus exams. I certainly did not shine academically and dismally failed the eleven plus not realizing or being told by my parents how important the results could be. Those with good marks went on to grammar schools, like Latimer Road, where the future was bright and could lead to higher education. We also-rans went to **Fulham Secondary School**. At the time it didn't seem important, life went on as normal but looking back it was a massive failure.

It was at this school that I learnt what a deterrent the 'cane' is. On one occasion, I must have committed a misdemeanor, the teacher sending me to the Head Master's office. You had to stand outside until you were called to enter. With fear and trepidation, I went in and stood in front of his desk. He gave some spiel about being a naughty boy, and then selected a cane from a rack and told me to hold out my hands, palm up. How many strokes depended on the severity of one's misdemeanor, mine must have been light as on each occasion it was only four strokes per hand. Also depending on his mood for the day, if OK the strokes came down central on the palm, otherwise they came down across the knuckles and that hurt even more. The main thing was, it hurt and taught me a lesson, never be naughty (or not get caught.) In my opinion the cane should be reintroduced. (Do gooders take note!)?

A New Zealand teacher meted out his own style of punishment and one time I witnessed him getting a boy to bend over his table, took the long blackboard ruler and whacked the boy across his buttocks to great mirth from the class when the ruler broke in half.

At a school medical I was diagnosed as having flat feet. This didn't worry me at all but later in life it was my exit from the army but that's another story.

Two good friends of mine at Sherbrook were Inky Kinch from Filmer Road who was a master footballer with a tennis ball and Digger Louch from Allestree Street a rather seedy part of Fulham. In the toilets one day with Digger I looked down, as one did, to compare sizes and was horrified by the sight. It was evident that he had never been told about personal cleanliness. Confused, do I tell him or just ignore? Being a good friend I gave him some good hygienic advice.

It was in these early days that I changed to long trousers, had a Boston haircut, very fashionable and had a first puff on a cigarette.

BALHAM & TOOTING COLLEGE OF COMMERCE

Having failed the 11 plus and going to down-market Fulham Secondary School, I had another chance to sit exams. Presumably I passed because we received a pamphlet setting out the details of various schools I could choose from. None were near Fulham but the one that caught my eye was in London's Hatton Gardens who specialize in diamond cutting. Dad advised I consider Balham & Tooting College of Commerce (BTCC), a school some 5 miles away just off Tooting Broadway in SW London, that could be reached by a direct 630 trolley bus ride. (This trolley bus was electric, connected to overhead cables). After an investigatory visit, I was accepted.

Sounds great, but in retrospect it was a poor school with no outside interests (e.g. no discussion groups, no training in the arts, no competitions against other schools and no drama or sports training).

FIRST DAY AT BTCC

First day was a total shock. Wandering around the playground the only ones I knew were Arthur Scutt and tiny Ernie Mills, both from Fulham Central (an all-boys school). However here there were masses of girls and we were all called to the main hall for allocating to classes. Off we all trudged thinking the boys and girls would be segregated but no such thing. There were 10 boys and 30 girls in my allocated class.

At home I announced to Mum that I didn't like the school and wanted to leave because there were so many girls. She, being the wise one, said just give it a trial and see how it pans out. Then I met friendly Kathleen Lloyd, a gorgeous, 5 feet 2, eyes of blue, such a happy face and figure to go with it, which changed my mind! We became quite a talking point. She appears in my amours appendix.

SCHOOL FRIENDS

My first close friend was Michael Josey nicknamed 'Wimpy', a small skinny chap with a keen sense of humour and we got on famously. Unfortunately, he contracted some illness and died aged about 15. I still have letters we swapped when he was in hospital. We made friends with Clancy, a powerfully built boy, who was at least 2 inches taller than me and looked 2 years older. Not that there was ever any bullying, but Clancy looked capable of scaring off even older boys. Don't know what happened to him, as he didn't return for the next year.

Pupils came from all over London and close friends were Norris Argyrou (known as "Archie") from Highbury, Stewart Chapman (known as "Fred") from Sheppard's Bush, Doug Hudson from Kings Cross, Arthur Richardson (known as "Ginge") from Stockwell and Mick Best from Chelsea.

Stewart's family came south from Northumberland when his father found it difficult to get work after the local mine closed, settled in S.W. London and he joined the police. About 1951 they retuned to a village named

Hazlerigg just north of Newcastle and it was there Stewart and some of us enjoyed summer holidays. It was on one of these holidays that he and I decided we would hitchhike west, over the Pennines Mountain Range heading for Cumberland. Trying to attract motorists our thumbs were extremely active but in a couple of days we had past Hexham, skirted Carlisle and reached our destination, Keswick where we lodged in a bed & breakfast and spent a couple of days wandering the shores of Derwent Water. More thumbing back to Hazlerigg.

We remained friends for life, unfortunately some lives were not so long, Doug who emigrated to Australia died about 1990 and only recently Stewart, Archie and Ginge passed away.

The GIRLS

Girls I fancied, in addition to Kathleen, were Anne Slade who played the accordion, Joan Wells, Gillian White, (all mentioned in the chapter of my Amours), Olga Povey, and Barbara Goodman. Some of who succumbed to my charms. As an aside, Barbara Goodman subsequently married Dennis Goodwin (long time acting partner of Bob Monkhouse, who married her friend Jacqueline Harding).

The TEACHERS

Of course teachers were all important. The only substandard teacher was old Mrs. Burns, who took us for Geography and History. She must have been in her 70s or 80s. Luckily, before we came up to the final year Mr. Hackett replaced her. What a revelation. On his first day he came into the classroom and just stood there while we decided to ignore him and went on chatting. He continued standing in front looking unconcerned and slowly the chatting died down and finally there was silence. He then said 'good morning' and told us about his war experiences in the tank corps. From then on he was the best teacher ever and without him I doubt if I would have passed these two subjects.

Our classroom had high vaulted ceiling with iron bars going across and one-day larking about after lessons, Stewart was swinging Tarzan like across the bars when headmaster, Mr. Bannan (known as Chic), entered the room and staring at Stewart said in a loud voice "Chapman what do you think you are doing." I think he saw the funny side as he just turned and walked out.

SCHOOL SPORTS

The sports afternoons were pathetic. First we had to catch a bus to Raynes Park, some 30-minute drive away, walk up a road 500 yards and then into this huge playing field. We had no coaching, and just kicked about in an unorganised football game. The only excitement was watching the girls play rounders in their navy blue knickers with vest tucked in. At the slightest chance of rain, it was cancelled. Mind you, I don't think I would have shined at any game, I could never do a handstand, or a cartwheel, climb a rope, run very fast or a distance but I did attempt many sports. As I came to remark, in all I tried I reached 'glorious mediocrity!'

GETTING IN TROUBLE

The 630 trolley bus was a good place for doing some homework, as Stewart caught the same bus to Hammersmith and Mick changed at Putney for Chelsea. Sometimes we'd discuss homework, but more likely we'd play pontoon. Pontoon became popular with the gang and a few shillings changed hands. More money changed hands when Doug and Mick started running a book on the horses, nothing too serious but it was 'strange' how they rarely lost. This stopped when they were found out and reprimanded.

At an evening after-school social, all the table tennis tables were full. So, with nothing else to do, Stewart, Mick, and I decided to climb over the wall into the rear of the adjacent billiard hall to look for a tennis ball we had kicked over there earlier in the day. It was pretty dark so we were rummaging about when we saw police with flashlights climbing over the intervening walls towards us. The other two hopped back over the wall pretty lively into the shed we had climbed on. I was a little slower but when I did get down I saw the two of them being frog-marched off by the police. Instead of being sensible and keeping schtum, I yelled out "What's going on?" At which point a policeman rushed back and frog-marched me to the others!

We were taken to Tooting Police Station and humorlessly questioned by the arresting officer and the station sergeant. We had to empty our pockets and when the sergeant saw my very small pair of nail scissors he held them up as though they were evidence of nefarious dark deeds! They would not listen to our story or phone the school as we suggested but promptly charged us with attempting to steal lead off the roof of the billiard hall. All our parents were contacted and they had to come and collect us. The police would not alter the charge so on the Friday, accompanied by our parents, we all had to go to Balham Juvenile Court. Quite intimidating. The judge sitting on high, listened to the police officer explain the crime. After only about 5 minutes of listening to the police, the judge said he was appalled at the waste of Court time, gave the police a dressing down and dismissed the case. So no criminal record (as yet!).

SCHOOL TRIPS TO THE THEATRE

I remember a school trip to the Lyric Hammersmith to see Paul Schofield, Eric Porter and Herbert Lomas in Richard III. Although, I have to say, the 'Classics' didn't grab me then and they don't grab me now.

Another school trip to the Lyric Hammersmith (I think) to see Romeo & Juliet. The only thing I remember is the beautiful Claire Bloom as Juliet leaning over the balcony displaying her ample bosom, a wonderful sight.

SCHOOL TRIPS ABROAD

My first trip abroad was the School trip to Bruges aboard The Prince Albert from Dover to Ostend, where I bought my first camera, a Baby Brownie for 18/-. (18 shillings in old money. 90p now)

On an outing to Brandenburg we got in trouble when Archie and I crashed the tandem we had hired. The language barrier meant lots of gesticulating with the angry owner. We tried to explain that we were sorry but had no money to recompense him. He was not a happy bunny.

Another incident occurred in a local café when we discovered that we were expected to pay for water. I declared "we never pay for water in England" and no matter the protestations the owner made I would not pay.

Anne Slade and Barbara Goodman where part of the party and with

Betty Jones from Brixton Grammar we had some good fun.

Visits to Dunkirk and Ghent Cathedral and pillow fights every night, it was the best holiday yet!

ACADEMIC ACHIEVEMENTS

Although I didn't think I was doing very well academically, my class position each year was in the upper quartile. So, after three years, when there was a selection process as to who should leave and who should go on to O levels, I was selected. Somehow I managed to pass all 7 subjects I took. The only one in the Year who didn't fail a subject (although some did pass 7, they had taken more). I didn't realise how important this was until I was taken under articles for a chartered accountant.

LAST DAY OF SCHOOL

21st July 1953. Last day of school. No build up. Nothing special. We just left our classrooms about midday and wandered into the playground where we hung around with friends wondering about what the big wide world offered us. No presentations, no prom balls, no well-wishing from teachers. Very sad really. Nowadays everyone seems to stay on for 'A' levels but this didn't seem to be an option, or the chance of university, which I think I would have enjoyed.

(It has now been torn down and a supermarket built)

****

My school days were interrupted on 11th July 1951 when my family moved to The Six Bells Pub in Colerne, Wiltshire, see separate chapter 6.

I often wonder how my life would have changed had I had the privilege of going to university. Listening to those of my grandchildren chatting about their experiences it sounds like a little work and much play. I am jealous. But in my day only the rich or landed gentry ever went to university.

CHAPTER 4

MY EARLY YEARS
&
BOYHOOD JOBS

The street, Ringmer Avenue in Fulham, was the playground for our small gang, John Deesie, a couple of years older than the rest was the unofficial leader, then there was his mate Shuttleworth, Beryl & Brian Davis, Babe Dodsworth, Janet Crane and Alex Drury that was until his house at number 33 was totally destroyed in a Jerry bombing raid. Then there was Harry Turner who lived in the next road and turned up in my life 64 years later. One dark night John Deesie led a group of us to Bishops Park, it was all locked up but somehow he got us in and we wandered towards the Putney Bridge end where there is a café. I don't know how but we got inside, it was very scary and I had no idea why we were there possibly hoping to find some cash when the burglar alarm went off. Brian and I ran like the devil was after us until we reached the safety of Fulham Palace Road. What a laugh John and the others had when they informed us that it was no burglar alarm just the fridge motor starting. Then I knew I would never be a burglar.

Must mention that Mr. Davis at number 13 had an incredible left hand drive American car, a Hudson Terraplane. All us kids were in awe. This was one of only 3 cars in the road at that time and we were annoyed if they interfered with our games of football, roller hockey and cricket where the centre manhole cover was the wicket. Now they double park. Then there were more sophisticated games like marbles and flick cards. Flick cards were in every pack of cigarettes that contained a variety of sets of such things as footballers, cricketers, military flags, motor cars, army regiments etc, all designed to encourage parent smokers to buy more packets to satisfy the needs of their children to complete a set. Some put them in albums, others swapped but the fun was a game of flicking them against a wall, if your card landed on another it was yours, quite upsetting if you lost one of your favourites.

They were also the first to have a television, a huge wooden box with a screen about 9 inches wide on which they hung a magnifying glass to enlarge the picture. Their children, Beryl & Brian would invite us in to watch but we found nothing interesting certainly no challenge to the radio with the likes of Dick Barton Special Agent that had us scuttling indoors at 6 p.m. to listen to his adventures with his buddies Jock & Snowy, The Man in Black scary stories narrated by Valentine Dial (Mum and I would sit in the dark getting chills up our spines). One episode stuck in my mind, Father and daughter were in a bungalow in the middle of a jungle, the girl was playing the piano when her father said "whatever you do, do not stop playing" as a python had got through the window and was approaching the piano. Silence as the snake slithered across the piano and disappeared. What a relief! Later it was the Goon Show.

THE BOY SCOUTS

I don't remember the name of the group but we met in a typical church hall in Harbour Street just up the road from Fulham Football Club. We met every Tuesday evening; I loved the games but was not keen on getting badges so much so that when they were desperate for another patrol seconder, I didn't qualify but as there was no one else I got my stripes. The games were great especially British Bulldog where the group was split in two, one each end of the hall. On the word 'go' each side charged the other with the object of getting to the other end first by whatever means possible. Being in charge of one team a young scout came to me complaining that that big boy over there had kicked him under the chin. Well I went over to remonstrate with this rather rolly polly lad and accused him of rough play. He was quite crest fallen and said "all I did was this" and with that he kicked me under the chin. No recriminations.

One of the most magical things about scouts was the summer camps, such happy days unless you were picked to dig the latrines or wash the breakfast pots and pans coated with dried porridge. One camp was near Looe in Cornwall and the journey there was something to behold. It was by an open backed lorry with canvas roof and sides. All our knap sacks, tents and other paraphernalia were piled on the back and about 20 of us jumped on board. During the 150-mile journey we enjoyed waving and cheering at passing motorists. (Don't know what Heath & Safety would make of it).

The campsite was a large field that sloped gently down towards the woods, tents were pitched, latrines dug and the Troop's Flag Pole raised. After a days troop parade and fun and games we sat round the camp fire singing scouty songs like 'Ging Gang Goolly Goolly Wat'cher Ging Gang Goo' and turned in about mid-night. In the dead of the night it started raining cats & dogs, no problem as we were nicely tucked up in our sleeping bags that was until about 3 a.m. when I felt a bit wet. I put out my arm and it went splash, my sleeping bag was soaking. I woke the others but their attitude was 'I'm all right jack' so I crept out and woke the scout master explaining my predicament. He found another sleeping bag and I spent the rest of the night in his tent. In the morning we investigated as to why only I got soaked. It turned out there was a narrow rut coming down the middle of the field and my place was the only one in it.

Looe is a quaint old Cornish town with a fast running stream running parallel to the narrow main street right down to the sea. A game we liked to play was each getting a stick we could recognize, throw them into the stream, it was then a race to see who got to the sea first.

I recommend all boys should experience the fun and comradeship you get from being a scout. Presumably it is the same for girls in the Girl Guides. Unfortunately, the media is now full of youngsters being molested fortunately I never experienced or witnessed anything untoward.

GUY FAWKS NIGHT & FIREWORKS

I had never known fireworks as they were banned during the war but only after two years there were festivities and fireworks. Parents in our road arranged a huge bonfire in the middle of the road and there was great anticipation as to what was to happen. I think this was a one-off occasion because in the morning the tar in the middle of the road had melted leaving a substantial scar. I had saved 12 shillings (6 new pence) from the earnings of my paper round (a fortune) and spent the whole lot on masses of fireworks, jumping jacks flashes where a group of us would hold hands in a circle that you had to be quick on your toes to avoid, Squids that were like torpedo's, Roman Candles that we attached to poles and used like rifles, Katherine wheels and my favourites BANGERS that when covered with a dustbin lid could toss it about 12 feet into the air.

One particularly eerie trip was to the railway bridge crossing the Thames from Fulham to Putney. It is hard to explain but parallel to the railway lines was a footpath with a railing to the right that we climbed over, ducked under the railway line onto the top of the huge supporting iron pillars where there was a type of well. From here we could look down on the river and here the squibs came into their own because when lit and dropped into the river they whizzed through the water at speed. It felt so thrilling listening to people walk overhead completely hidden. Presumably it is still possible to do this, why not give it a go?

PAPER ROUND. 10th June 1949 started morning paper round at old man Parsons newsagents on the corner of Munster Road and Burntwood Avenue. I got the cushiest round, Ferndown Road only about 60 houses for which I got a weekly pay of 12/6p a week (65p). Wealth. The shop was like a dim Aladdin's confectionary cave; large glass jars on shelves around the room filled with humbugs and many different sweets. Chocolates of every description and a counter behind which old man Parsons would welcome customers. By the time I got to the shop about 7a.m. he had marked up the papers for every round ready for us boys (never any girls) to venture into the early morning world. Later I also took on an evening round, in retrospect this was a bad move because it meant I had to leave school promptly thereby missing after school activities.

Going to my paper round one Sunday morning there in the gutter was a 10-shilling note (50p), wealth indeed. The thought of handing it in soon disappeared. I phoned my mate Mick who lived in Chelsea, caught the 14 bus, picked him up at Beauford Street and headed for London's West End. First something to eat, then what do we do with this fortune? Decided on the cinema to see Harold Lloyd (an old silent movie star) in Mad Wednesday. Can't remember what it was about but do remember him hanging off the arms of Big Ben. Ice creams then bus home with still a little change in my pocket.

Bob-a-Job. Although not earning money I include Bob-a-Job week while in the scouts. Presumably for charity we had to knock on doors and ask if there were any jobs we could do for a BOB (this was a shilling in old money now 5p). This taught me a good lesson; the richer people are the harder it is to get them to part with money. For example, going round Fulham, a working class area, you might be asked to clean a pair of shoes or pop round to the corner shop for an item or two and might even get a couple of Bob. Then I thought, those big houses up Putney Hill, they must be rich so off I went. The first job was to cut the garden hedge some 30 feet long. Took over an hour, thought this will be good for a few bob. None of it, just the one. Next I had to mow a large lawn of a big house with the same result, so it was back to Fulham.

MILK ROUNDS. About this time, I started working for Mr. Owen a Welshman who owned the dairy shop at the end of Ringmer Avenue. Early each morning a lorry would deliver large churns of milk and my job was to ladle out milk and fill various size milk bottles, seal them with cardboard caps then put them into crates and load the crates onto his push cart before we set off on his round. But in 1950 I left him for the allure of working with Jack the milkman (who smoked incessantly right down to a bare stub) the opening being because Reg, who worked with him for a couple of years, left to join the navy. The attraction was that he had a horse & cart from the Express Dairy. It was with him that I learnt to carry 5 bottles of empties in each hand. Four shillings a week. The real excitement was after a long day collecting money on a Saturday, Jack let the horse, which had just trudged round all day, have free reign and head for the stable. It was like Ben Hur as he galloped home to the Express Dairy near Putney Bridge.

GREENGROCERS. 18th July 1952 Stewart and I started a Saturday job for Mr. & Mrs. Costanzos in their greengrocery shop near Cottismere Gardens in the back streets of London's upmarket Knightsbridge shopping area, for £3.5.0 per week each. Our friend Mick who worked next door in the butchers, had got us the job but was upset when he learnt we earned more than him. Mr. Costanzo aged about 50 had a potbelly, invariably had a pipe in his mouth and spent the whole day going around tunelessly humming. His wife, a few years younger looked like a renegade from a B movie one of those down trodden wives who lived in the midwest. Presumably at some stage she might have been quite a looker but would never get more than 5 out of 10 for presentation. Then there was mother who was in her dotage, never seen without a cigarette drooping from the centre of her mouth, never coming out so the smoke used to drift right up over her nose, her eyebrows and the middle of her hair, such that she had this brown streak the whole way up her face that Stewart and I thought hysterical.

Stewart and I were always fighting over who was going to do the deliveries on this old trade bike with a basket at the front. One day I won but the first load was a sack of potatoes, too heavy for him to lift high, I leant the bike over so he could haul the sack onto the basket while I held the bike steady. Plonk went the sack, the bike tilted, I tried to straiten the bike, it didn't move but the handlebar stem bent so it was a very wonky ride. One day Mr. Costanzo, a weedy looking individual, asked Stewart to go to the hardware shop just around the corner to buy some skyhooks and a rubber hammer. He returned saying the shopkeeper told him they were out of the skyhooks but was expecting a delivery of rubber hammers next week.

The whole set up of the shop was totally new to us, a real Aladdin's Cave stocked with so many fruits and vegetables we had never seen, curly kale, spring greens, squashes, cloves of garlic etc. Stewart asked Mr. Costanzo what this white small thing was. "Try it" said Mr. C. so Stewart popped it into his mouth had just one bite, spat it out and ran round the shop having bites of apples and anything else that would cool his mouth. It was a clove of garlic.

As time went by we progressed to being able to serve in the shop, we saw this as pretty senior stuff and got pleasure dealing with most customers. However, there were exceptions particularly an old lady she rarely spent more than a shilling or two and would engage the server prattling on about something totally trivial and of no interest to us teenagers.

Well on this particular day she was sighted approaching so a mad dash into the back. I think Mr. Costanzo tripped me up because I was last man standing. She came in carrying a small saucepan with lid on. She came up to me and said "young man I wonder whether you could help me, only I don't know whether this is alright to eat" where upon she lifted the lid. I peered in and there at the bottom was some mucky looking goo. "Yes madam it looks fine but I think you should hurry home and cook it now".

We stayed at Costanzos until we left school and then it was out into the wide world.

TEENAGE ME　　　　　　*ON BABE'S BIKE*

MICK INFRONT OF WIMPY ICE SKATING

CHAPTER 5

A CHILD'S HAPPY MEMORIES OF THE WAR YEARS

EVACUATION – PHASE 1

War was declared on 1st September 1939. It soon became clear that the government thought that Hitler intended to bomb us (specifically London and major industrial areas). As a precaution the Government bought in Evacuation. This meant that children under 8 with their mums and children over 8 on their own had to leave built up areas and move out to the comparative safety of the countryside.

First of us to go was Reg, then 9 or 10 years old with his little suitcase, gas mask and a few coppers, off to God knows where. (Believe it or not parents weren't informed!!!!)

Mum and I were billeted with a Mr. & Mrs. Puttick in Worplesdon, Surrey. So Dad loaded up his Morris 8, and off we went on the short 30-mile trip. Other evacuees were sent to far off places like North Wales and even as far as Canada.

They were a very old couple that had a son away in the army so they had a spare room. They made us welcome and fixed us up in their tiny cottage.

We were allocated our chores, and one unpleasant duty allocated to Mum was toilet duty. There was no internal toilet and the toilet shed in the garden had no sewerage, so the bucket had to be taken regularly to the end of the garden, a hole dug (always hoping it was a new one!), and the contents buried.

We had no idea where Reg had been sent but one day Mum took me to the cattle market in Guildford and strolling along towards us was Reg! Mum was ecstatic and much embracing followed. Apparently he was staying with a loving couple nearby that treated him like a son (he visited them many times after the war).

EVACUATION – PHASE 2

Anyway Hitler didn't send bombers that time so, after only a few months, back we came. However, Hitler eventually made good his threat and started his bombing campaign in late 1940. The campaign was known as The Blitz.

So we went back to the Puttick's (this time with Reg in tow). Right across the road was a huge common, with loads of ferns to hide in, trees to climb and wide-open spaces to explore. Reg and his friends dug a shelter. Such a difference from built up Fulham with its terraced houses and only Bishop's Park as a place with trees in which to play.

BEACH HUTS

About 1940, Dad got a letter from the War Office saying beach huts could be used by the Germans if they invaded, so either remove them or they will be blown up by order of the Government. Naturally Dad removed his one at Whitstable (temporarily).

The BOMBING OF LONDON (1939)

War breaking out meant nothing to a 3 years old and the only memory I have before we moved from Atlanta Street was one night when Jerry dropped incendiary bombs on Kingwood Road School in the next road to us. It went up in flames that could be seen for miles around and from my bedroom window we got a ringside view of the flames over the rooftops. I was all for going round and getting a closer look, but Dad considered this a danger.

Fearing for our safety, Dad borrowed the next-door neighbours son's bike, cycled to Earls Court Exhibition Centre (about 5 miles away, where he worked) as he had his Morris 8 parked there. Then he drove back, collected the four of us and back to Earls Court to spend the rest of the night in the underground tunnels of the Exhibition Centre.

BLACKOUTS

For fear of giving German pilots any idea of towns and cities there were to be no sign of lights hence all road lighting was off and houses had to cover their windows so that no light whatsoever showed outside. There were Air Raid Wardens who patrolled the streets and would warn any offenders.

RATIONING

Rationing was introduced in January 1940. First for just a few essential items, but gradually it encompassed many things and even those items that were not rationed could be in short supply.

Everyone was issued with a ration book that had coupons. These were then used to buy goods. Although I remember it was quite exciting handing over a coupon or two to buy a few sweets, it was extremely tough on the housewives trying to feed a family.

The idea was to make supplies fair to everyone. However, dubious persons (commonly known as 'Spivs') found ways to get more than their fair share. Not necessarily for their own use, but to sell on the black market to the highest bidders.

Rationing didn't finally end until 4th July 1954, when meat and bacon became available.

Imports pre-war were 20 million tonnes, 70% of our cheese & sugar, 80% of our fruits, 70% of our cereals & fats and 100% of our petrol. Most of this coming across The Atlantic constantly harassed by German U boats. Unimaginable how we survived. Good old Churchill.

The 'DIG FOR VICTORY' CAMPAIGN

The Government also encouraged people to 'Dig for Victory' by growing their own vegetables. Dad, in a weak moment, signed up for an allotment (although he had never put a spade in the ground in his life!). He tried to get Reg and me to help, but this fell on deaf ears. Consequently, we only went there on the odd occasion. As I recall all we got were a cauliflower and some peas.

Bernard Pendry

The BOMBING OF LONDON (1943)

As the war continued on (the war in Europe didn't officially end until May 1945) I remember an occasion where a message went round that there was a basket of unexploded incendiary bombs in the alleyway behind the shops in Fulham Road. So off we cycled, as fast as we could, to beat the authorities. And, lo and behold, there was what looked like a tin bath loaded with bombs! But before we could get any closer, the fire brigade arrived and shooed everyone away to a safe distance. Looking back, it was probably for the best!

Every morning on the way to school or just playing in the road there was a search for shrapnel (those jagged pieces of metal, the result of exploded bombs). Oh where did my stash of shrapnel go?

Teachers at school had told us all about Doodle Bugs (Germany's first unmanned rockets) that we may see in the sky because of the rockets flame and the distinct buzzing sound. But when the buzzing stopped and the flame went out, it would take 10 seconds for it to land and explode. Well a gang of us were playing games in Ringmer Avenue when the cheer went up "Look there's a doodle bug" and clear enough we could see and hear it. Then nothing. So as we had been told, we all dived behind the copings and counted back from 10, 9, 8, 7, 6, 5, 4, 3, 2. 1. BOOM! Windows shattered, roof tiles came down, but thankfully nothing more. The bomb had landed six streets away and demolished nearly every house in that street!

I don't know from where, but one of the gang had found a bottle of phosphorous that, when poured, glowed a bright yellow. Well this could be fun we thought. We selected a house that had the lights on, crept up to the front door, poured some phosphorous on to the front mat, knocked on the door and hastily ran across the road and dived behind some bushes to watch. Quite entertaining to watch an occupant open the door, scratch his head in wonder, then calling out the rest of the family to look at the eerie glow.

THE ANDERSON AIR RAID SHELTER

It must have been around 1940, when a gang of workmen turned up at our house, no doubt with legal papers, to erect an Anderson Air-raid Shelter and promptly begun digging a hole in our back garden.

The hole seemed enormous to me in our postage stamp of a garden, but it was about 3 feet deep and masses of concrete was used to make a solid floor, then galvanised corrugated steel sheets were inserted, semi-circular, so they joined at the top. These were supposed to be excellent protection against a bomb blast, but what amuses me is that the front door was made of thin wood that could have been blown in with a puff of wind. Anyway when the air-raid sirens did go off, it was a quick trip to the shelter. I found the shelter to be surprisingly snug and comforting. These shelters were made to sleep 6 and my bed was across the rear end of the shelter (prime position!). When the 'All Clear' siren sounded, it was back indoors.

However, on one occasion, when alighting from the shelter, there, lying in the garden, was an unexploded incendiary bomb. This could have brought panic to the bravest of people, but Dad just put a dustbin lid on it and said "Alice, I have to go on Home Guard Duty so just keep an eye on it" and with that, off he went to inspect what damage had been caused!

That night the Drury's house was destroyed and an incendiary bomb had gone through the roof of the Davis's house, but luckily burnt itself out on their bed, doing no further damage.

I don't recall how or when we got rid of our shelter, but many years later Ray Saunders and I helped Ted Pemble (Sheila's dad) remove their Anderson Shelter in his garden. It took us days and much muscle to get the thing out of the ground!

METAL FOR THE WAR EFFORT

The War Office decided that all available metal was needed for the war effort. So one day, another gang of workers came with oxyacetylene torches and cut off every iron railing on the copings and front garden gates. These were quite unique and were never replaced. There is a rumour that the metal was never used.

Bernard Pendry

WAR ENDS IN EUROPE

On 9th May 1945 (with Hitler having committed suicide in his bunker ten days before) Germany surrendered.

Great celebrations took place all over the country. Every street had a party. Ours was no exception. It was great! Everyone down the street contributed something. Tables and chairs were lined down the center of the road and became festooned with food, cakes, pies, sandwiches, jellies and drinks. They must have used many ration coupons!

Number 33 the home of the Drury's had been raised to the ground by a bomb, so this made an ideal place to erect a makeshift stage upon which loads of neighbours got up and did a turn, not least my Dad. He loved to sing all the old songs, especially Flannigan and Allen (his favourites). They tried to get me up to sing my kids party piece, 'Boiled Beef and Carrots'. I was last seen running round the corner at the end of the street!

VICTORY IN JAPAN

Not long after, on 15th August 1945 (following the bombing of Hiroshima on 6th August) the Japanese also surrendered. And the war was finally over.

So… another lavish street party.

The downside was seeing the newsreels of the horrors of Belsen (one of the German concentration camps) and the Japanese concentration camps (with those that survived looking like living skeletons). These images live with you forever. Can we now return to normal? No way. Our perspectives have changed and many people, of my parent's generation, and mine can never forgive or forget what the Germans and Japs did.

RANDOM POST WAR DATES

3rd April 1949: Lights come on in London for the first time since the war.

25th April 1949: Sweets finally come off of rationing (great news to a 13 year old!)

7th May 1949: Fulham F.C beat West Ham 2-0 to win the league.

In November 1949, Reg joined the Navy on HMS Truelove. My big brother told me lots of stories on his frequent home leaves.

Also in 1949, Dad got permission to erect another beach hut to replace the one taken down before the war.

CHAPTER 6

THE SIX BELLS PUB, COLERNE, WILTSHIRE

Dad's close friend, Reg Swift had retired from mainstream work and with wife had bought a pub just south west of Bath, famous for the well preserved Roman Baths . We visited this pub a few times and Dad so enjoyed serving behind the bar he got it into his head that he should try the same thing. So in early 1950 he bought The Six Bells Pub in Colerne in Wiltshire (pronounced Coln) and on 11th July we left Ringmer Avenue and set out west.

The pub was really quaint and had been a resting stop for pilgrims on their way to Canterbury as it was on high ground between Bath and Chippenham. The walls were about 18 inches thick and the large cellar was honed out of solid chalk rock hence being ideal for keeping the beer at the perfect temperature. Out the back was a rustic shed housing a nine pin bowling alley where the local team played every week. This was nothing like modern bowling alleys, the knocked down pins had to be replaced by hand and the wooden balls placed in a wooden chute to return. The person doing this got a few tips and even more when they had to go into the pub and get the beer order. I thoroughly enjoyed these nights.

There was one bus in the morning into Bath that returned at 5 p.m.. If you missed either it was hard luck. A travelling fish & chip van came on Fridays; occasionally there was a travelling film show in the Village Hall.

Of course I had to leave BTCC and they found me a place at a peculiar mixed school in Bath, when I say mixed there were only 2 other boys. All I remember was sports afternoons, we boys had the choice of going to games or having spare time, they stayed I went with the girls. Traditionally our girls played hockey against another girls school and regularly got beaten. Now I knew nothing about hockey but took to it well and imposed my superior strength, got used to using the stick (silly thing that you could only use one side) and after being told I couldn't shoot from outside the arc we started winning.

The Six Bells was a focal point in the village although there was another pub and a social club along the high street. I soon got to know the local boys who I played football with but got on much better with the girls, especially Zena Alford and Pat Shadbolt fondly remembered. (Read My Amours)

Our stay didn't last long, possibly 8 months, all this time Ringmer had been on the market for sale. One day Dad come back and said to Mum "Al at last we have an offer to sell. So do we sell or go home?" There was no hesitation "Yes let's go home". Mum had hated her role as Dad kept his London job and spent only weekends in the pub, leaving Mum to run the place mid week. She had no idea what she was doing especially working out the money side. Typically an old mentally challenged aristocratic gent who lived in the parsonage would enter the pub at opening time, order a half pint of ale then proceed to engage Mum in some useless banter while she had work to do. She was so thrilled to be going back to Fulham.

I think the locals must have been pleased to see us go because Dad was a rotten publican. The previous governor used to have after's especially for the soldiers who had a camp not far away and regularly invited the governor back to their camp for a late drink. Dad had none of this so prompt at closing time he would start sweeping from the far end and putting chairs on the tables. To anyone who complained he would say, "Do you do overtime for no pay?"

Twice I cycled from Fulham to Colerne and back, a round trip of over 200 miles. On my first ride I stopped at a café in Hungerford and was enchanted to hear Guy Mitchell sing *She Wears Red Feathers and a Hoola Hoola Skirt* thought it was one of the best tunes I ever heard. Reaching the village of Box it was left turn and 2 or 3 miles up hill to Colerne

On the last trip home we loaded my bike onto the back of Dad's Morris 8 but before leaving I was asked to put on a rear wheel, that had just been mended, onto the car. Approaching Hungerford the car started to wobble and swerve all over the place. Quick stop: the reason was clear, the wheel I had fitted had come loose and sheared the bolts, obviously I hadn't tightened them securely. I thought Dad would throw a wobbly but he was very understanding and told me to get my bike off the car and cycle the rest of the way while he called a garage.

So it was back to Balham & Tooting College of Commerce

DAD THE GOVERNER OF THE 6 BELLS PUB

COLERNE HIGH STREET

ME AS TEENAGER

CHAPTER 7

EMPLOYMENTS AFTER EDUCATION

Like most of my contemporaries we had no idea of what we wanted but having attended a commercial college it was obvious we would end up office bound. I don't think "Unemployment" was in the dictionary and everyone seemed to have a job to go to. The vision seemed to be 'let's get a job to earn some money and hopefully have a future'.

MY FIRST JOB

My first job was as a junior clerk at an insurance brokers in The Minories, in The City of London. All I can remember of this job was masses of thick files with insurance policies that had to be filed in these sliding cabinets that went back about 4 rows. The only other memory was when a fellow clerk came back in from the loo and said, "Have you seen what is in the loo". Not to go into detail but they had to call out the janitor.

MY 2ⁿᵈ JOB: JOCELYN MILES – CHARTERED ACCOUNTANTS

In hindsight, the insurance broker job was probably going nowhere. Luckily Dad came to my rescue. At the time he was working at Debenhams Departmental Store in Oxford Street and his boss, Bill Overton a chartered accountant, got me an interview with Jocelyn Miles, a firm of chartered accountants in the City.

The interview was at their offices in Kings Street, opposite The Guild Hall in The City of London. Not only had I never been to the City, but also I didn't even know what chartered accountants did. So, as you can imagine, I was a little nervous. The offices were Dickensian; dark panelled woodwork, dingy staircase, and thick patterned carpet and there, sitting behind a large imposing leather inlayed oak desk, sat old Mr. Campbell. He had a small, stiff white collar, tie and obligatory dark waist coated suit. However, despite my nerves, he made me most welcome. He asked me a few questions about accountancy, to which I did not know the answers, asked if I was prepared to work hard, to which the answer was a definite "yes" (what idiot would say "Not on your Nelly?)

Anyway he must have taken a liking to me, because he offered me the chance to go under 5 years articles, with a view to eventually becoming a chartered accountant. He went on to explain that until a year or two ago, parents had to pay for their children to be accepted under articles with no pay. Now I would get £3 p.w. for the first 2 years, rising to £4 p.w. for the next 2 years and the mighty sum of £5 p.w. for the final year. As I was earning £3.15.0d at the insurance company it didn't seem too bad.

He gave me a wonderful piece of advice: "Study for 3 hours every weekday evening, without exception, but never at weekends. This is your time for socialising". I took this to heart and kept to it religiously throughout my studying years with only a few exceptions like an invite for a theatre trip or an interesting party.

I joined Jocelyn Miles on 29th October 1953 and thus started 5 years hard study whilst also working full time. I think I was fortunate to have the opportunity, as all my contemporaries were ex public school.

OFFICE DRESS CODE

My ex-public school contemporaries had no problem with the expected dress code: traditional bowler hat, white shirt with stiffened collar, pin striped waist coated dark suit and appropriate tie, accompanied by rolled umbrella and leather brief case.

I did conform to most of this, but I couldn't bring myself to sport a bowler hat (as most of the others did) however I did treat myself to a trilby that I steamed so the brim curled upwards. Very trendy (or so I thought!) My rolled umbrella came from Foxes in Holborn. You folded it as tight as possible and used it in a military fashion when walking along the road.

My first hand-made suit came from Childs in Wandsworth High Street. What a pleasant experience, choosing the material and type of cut. This was the start of a few years of hand made suits.

WORKING IN THE CITY

I could have been over awed by the whole city scene but took to it like a duck to water, never feeling inferior to the better educated colleagues. We got on well and it was a pleasant place to work.

We were given Luncheon Vouchers that you could use daily for a bite of lunch. Some saved them for a more elaborate meal. I don't think they are in use now.

MY FIRST AUDIT

My first out of town audit was to an iron foundry in Halifax. I caught a Sunday train from Kings Cross, to be ready for work on the Monday.

Alighting from the train, my first impression was that the town was covered in smoke. But on the bus ride to the factory, the smoke departed and just after a mile or so there was beautiful countryside.

With the manager, Mr. Lelman, a sartorial impressive dresser, we stayed at a three star hotel in the middle of the town. This was the first hotel I had ever been into. Dinner was served in a sparsely furnished room, with about 12 tables. No music, just the sound of clicking cutlery. The whole experience was new to me.

I got through the starter and main course OK by watching the cutlery used by my manager. When it came to the cheese and crackers course (Crawford's, I believe), I thought this is easy. First I put a cracker on my hand and attempted to spread the butter. The cracker divided into two. Then four. Ending in a fistful of crumbs! Well this tickled my sense of humour and I just burst out in fits of laughter to the embarrassment of Mr. Lelman and gasps from the other diners.

One lunchtime we went for a walk and approaching an avenue of trees he said "I'm not going down there, too many birds". After saying "don't be silly", down we wondered. 'Splat' a huge bird's droppings slid down the lapel of his incredibly fashionable suit. I don't think he was pleased! (Read My Amours about the waitress).

COMMUTING

Halifax aside, most of the audit jobs were in and around London and commuting could be a pain. So I decided to invest in a 150cc Vespa and used this most days. It was a nice journey into work, but the cobble stoned road surface was a bit slippery going around the Tower of London.

The CLIENTS

The 5 years under articles passed pleasantly enough, with my time mostly spent working out of the office, visiting various clients. Our clients included: Ever Ready, where I witnessed the most repetitive job possible, small light bulbs came round on a conveyor belt upside down with the two wires poking up, all the ladies, about 10 in the row, just had to twist the two wires together as they passed: Swan & Edgar departmental store in Piccadilly Circus (now a music store), one of the jobs was observing stocktaking and making a report that included 'the widows were perfect'"of course I meant windows: Bourne & Hollingsworth in Oxford Street and occasionally I had to raise a query with a director whose offices were on the 6th floor, it was like hallowed ground, thick pile carpet and not a sound to be heard; Bretles, in Belper, Derbyshire famous makers of gloves, and lots more.

ACCOUNTANCY EXAMS

I failed the first attempt at the Intermediate exam. I think this was because I was so far ahead of my studies that I went off the boil. No such problem with the next attempt and I came 145 out of 2000 odd.

I studied really hard for the Final exam. This was held in Central Hall, Westminster. Quite daunting. With hundreds of candidates sitting in rows, with three adjudicators watching over us. I thought I had done reasonably well but the results would not be made known for a few weeks.

You were informed the results would be posted and knew the post they would arrive in. It was a Saturday, first post normally arriving at 7.30. At 7.25 I sat on the bottom rung of the stairs, staring intently at the letterbox. You knew if you had passed, as the contents would be white. If failed, the contents would be yellow. 'Plop', the envelope hit the doormat. With trembling fingers I prised a corner of the envelope open… I let out a yell of jubilation. It was white! Mum & Dad came down so excited to congratulate me.

This was 24th January 1959. My salary was increased from £5 per week to the princely sum of £1,100 per annum. Again wealth untold.

But, just as my professional life was taking off, my call up papers arrived and it was off to the army! [See Chapter 8]

MY 21ST

CHAPTER 8

IN & OUT OF THE ARMY IN THREE WEEKS

CONSCRIPTION & DEFERRAL

Although the two years conscription was still well in force when I reached 18, as I was studying to become a chartered accountant I had been granted a 5-year deferral. However after 5 years the piper had to be paid. So there I was at the ripe old age of 23, having just qualified and earning the princely sum of £1,100 p.a., with a new wife, having to leave it all behind.

I fancied being wing Commander Pendry so applied to be sent to the Royal Air Force. However, they ignored that and instead they drafted me into the Green Jackets, the infantry regiment with the fastest marching pace in the world! I was told to report to their barracks at Winchester. Thursday 21ˢᵗ January 1960 there were tears from my new bride with her Mum and Dad on Waterloo Station with promises to send food parcels and to write frequently. Heaven knows what it must be like if I was going off to war! In a perverse way I was looking forward to 2 years of doing something different.

Somewhere along life's path I had learnt that I had flat feet, possibly some ancient school medical, so when I went for the first medical I let this fact be known in the forlorn hope that I wouldn't be accepted. It wasn't that I didn't want to fight for Queen and country but conscription had ended, there were no wars going on so what was the point? Anyway, I was passed A1 and even on appeal (i.e. a second medical) I was found to be a perfect specimen (well Sheila could have told them that!)

ARMY LIFE

I was expecting the archetypal bellowing Sergeant Major but in actual fact it was a fairly tame affair, just 3 corporals who strode around as though they owned the place. The shorter of the corporals was a quiet type but the other two, both about 6'2" tall, strode up and down the communal hut intimidating the new recruits by throwing a huge Bowie like knife into the wooden floor. It was a wonder they could see where they were going as the peaks of their caps went straight down over their eyes. Also I was the only recruit who had been deferred; therefore my barrack fellows were all 18, which seemed quite juvenile to a seasoned 23 years old!

First morning we were all kitted out with what they termed *third best battle dress*. In reality it resembled sackcloth. An officer would interview each of us in turn attempting to get us to sign on for a longer term. When he learnt of my situation he didn't try too hard saying it was a fun life for anyone who liked playing games. From then on we were taught how to march, lay out our kit for inspection, and how to get over an assault course. At the first assault course some of the recruits complained how difficult it would be to get over the brick wall so the nice corporal in his nice pressed uniform said "Watch me I'll show you how easy it is" and with that he took off at a fast run and launched himself at the brick wall, about the height of a vaulting horse, his foot slipped and he went head first into the wall like a bullet, catching his front teeth on the leading edge. Well when he picked himself up it was not a pretty sight; his two top front teeth had broken in two. Of course nobody laughed! It just shows not to be the nice guy.

EXITING THE ARMY

After about a week, I started to hear stories of recruits working their ticket and getting discharged for a variety of reasons, such as bed-wetting. Well, I didn't fancy that but I thought I'd try the flat feet card again so decided to report to the medical orderly. To do so you had to clean all your gear and lay it out in perfect order for inspection. This nearly put me off but the thought of possibly getting back to Sheila and a 'high' paying job spurred me on.

A final decision was beyond the medical orderly at Winchester, so he arranged a pass for me to visit the Medical Officer at Aldershot, the foremost army base in England. On the appointed day I got togged up in the only clothes we had been issued and reported to the guardhouse. Out came an officious corporal, one who had his cap over his eyes, he strutted around me a few times exclaimed, "Blimey, what we got here" and marched off to call out the duty sergeant. Their conversation proceeded as follows: Corporal "ain't he a mess we certainly cannot let him go out" Sergeant "But he's got a pass so we have to let him go but at least send him back to put his belt on". This was the most intelligent conversation I had heard by anyone from the armed forces.

The trip to Aldershot was quite daunting. Arriving there in my sub standard third best battle dress when every other soldier was spruced up and looking like proper soldiers, I felt a proper Charlie. After a few timid enquiries I eventually found the MO's office only to learn that he was away on a few days leave. Therefore the process was repeated a few days later. When I eventually met with the MO, he turned out to be a most understanding individual. The conversation went something like this – Me: "I told them at the original medical, that I had flat feet but they put me in this fast marching regiment. Now the problem is, that if I am downgraded, it will spoil my chances of a commission and if I cannot get a commission I'd rather not be in the forces" MO – "Mmmm, I see. Yes, in that case, you're out." Me: (with startled expression) "You mean I am getting out of the forces?" MO – "Yes" and that was that.

Back at Winchester, I was seconded to the office of the RSM (Regimental Sargent Major) who gave me the exciting job of unravelling a huge mangled ball of nametags. These were tin tags on a piece of string that all soldiers had to wear round their necks for identification if they got killed. It took about half hour to unwind just one! However I was rescued after about a day when he learnt that I could type. So for the days up to my release I acted as his secretary.

From start to finish I was in the army for a total of 21 days. Not only did I get the regular pay but later family allowance and even later came a cheque for demob pay.

AN ARMY SIDE NOTE

A few years later, my mate Ginge and I met for a drink after work in a pub just south of London Bridge and would you believe it the barman was ex Green Jackets just retired after 25 years. It was early evening and we were the only customers so we got chatting about army life. Ginge swears I had more stories from my 3 weeks than the barman did from his 25 years!

Was there anything the army taught me? Yes. How to put a really good shine on a pair of boots. lots of spit, a cloth with some polish on and then endless hours of tiny circles followed by the hot handle of a spoon. So there.

CHAPTER 9

EMPLOYMENTS AFTER THE ARMY

Once my 21 days in the army were over (see Chapter 8), I returned to Jocelyn Miles (chartered accountants) for another year or so. Then, still in the profession, I went to work for Kemp Chatteris, a larger firm.

More auditing didn't excite me, so I decided to get out of the profession altogether and into commerce. I thought that the manager I worked under at Kemp Chatteris would be a bit upset, but when I told him I was leaving, his reaction was "Bernard you are doing the right thing and always remember that nobody looks after you as well as you can do yourself". I took this to heart as a profound statement.

On 9th January 1963, I attended an interview at Gothic Press, a family business situated just south of London Bridge and had a very enjoyable meeting with a couple of their directors. They offered me the position of finance manager at a salary of £4,000 p.a. that I accepted.

Unfortunately, as it turned out, the next day I had another interview, which was to change my life. And not for the better!

The HUNNISETT ERA (1963–1972)

THE INTERVIEW

On 10th January, I met with Charles Hunnisett and his son Derek in their small office over their jewelers shop, just off Trafalgar Square. They gave me the whole schpiel about how they would be shortly moving into palatial offices in Camelford House, a 17 storey office block they had built just south of Vauxhall Bridge. They said that the future would be exciting, with possible directorship and share options going forward. (What a load of old b…ks).

Well I fell for their presentation and on 4th February 1963 I became the accountant for South Bank Estates Limited (SBE). For the next 9 years I shared a huge (but rather bare) office with Mr. Mate, the company secretary (a most delightful person). There were only two other employees, a receptionist and their secretary.

CAMELFORD HOUSE

Camelford House was 17 floors high, the first 15 floors already let to the Post Office at a very nice rent. The offices were on the 17th floor and the 16th floor housed a magnificent London residence for the Hunnisett family. More opulent than anything I had seen before. In the middle was an atrium, rising right up through the 17th floor housing a tropical garden. Fantastic! The reason that the residence was not on the top floor was because the lift only went to the 16th.

I was soon appointed registered key holder because I was the only senior person other than Mr. Mate who lived in Essex and the Hunnisett's who certainly didn't want to be disturbed in Brighton.

I wasn't too keen on the idea of being called out at any time however the good thing about this arrangement was that I could invite family and friends to come and see their palatial residence that I used a few times for special family and friends.

From the 17th floor you could get onto the flat roof with magnificent views over London. There were no railings just a 6-inch high parapet. So getting anywhere near the edge caused vertigo and a fear of being dragged over. The only way to look down was to crawl on ones stomach and just peer over the edge. Even then it was scary.

We had the whole of the top floor, but the offices only occupied about a third. The rest was just empty space where sometimes I would practice my squash shots. Mr. Mate and myself shared a large office whilst both Mr. Hunnisett and his son Derek had well appointed offices having views of the Thames and Vauxhall Bridge.

The BOARD OF DIRECTORS

The board of directors of SBE was impressive: a young Jacob Rothschild (now Lord), Jack Hughes (now a Sir) a senior partner in the estate agents firm of Jones, Lang and Wotton and Sir Eric Proudfoot head partner in the firm of Denton, Hall and Burgin solicitors plus the Hunnisett's

The board room was just as impressive, a large oak table with inlaid blue leather matched by high backed arm chairs with views over the Thames: to the right the Houses of Parliament; to the left, Battersea Power Station. It was such a good view that one day a young lady called and asked if she would be allowed to paint the scene. Much to my surprise Mr. H readily agreed and a week later she produced an incredible painting.

After the board meetings the directors would go off for lunch to some exotic restaurant, leaving Mr. Mate and myself to do the clearing up. Well not literally!

LUNCH

Lunch times, I sometimes wandered down to the Post Office canteen on the 13th floor and there I met Jerry and Ann both fine bridge players who taught me how to play. And one of these relationships continued for many years, it was not Jerry.

EMERGENCY CALL OUT

One Saturday morning, as registered key holder, I received a phone call from the tenants on the 15th floor informing me that water was dripping through their ceiling. I enquired how bad it was; to which the reply was that is was only a few drips. I suggested they put a bucket under, which they had already done. Not thinking it was serious (and not wanting to disturb my weekend) I did nothing until the Monday morning.

Well, first thing Monday morning I entered the flat, took one step inside and "splash". The whole of the hallway was under water that was rising up the expensive wall coverings and going into adjoining rooms. On investigation I found what had happened the chauffer (whose name escapes me), who had the task of looking after the tropical garden, had been watering it on the Friday before Mr. H and Derek headed home to Brighton and forgot to turn the water off. It shouldn't have been a problem, but a build up of leaves had blocked the drain.

Anyway, what to do? A major problem was that in 4 weeks time the Duke of Cornwall, who owned the freehold, was due to visit for the grand opening of the building. Straight away I phoned Mr. H. telling him the problem but leaving out the Saturday phone call (thinking he would explode). But calmly he just said to get onto the insurers and let them sort it out. And they did an excellent job such that the grand party (I am told) went well.

BIG PROJECTS

Derek and Mr. H were forever searching the Estates Gazette for likely acquisitions which first resulted in buying a site in Croydon with planning permission to build a 7 storey high office block. This was a new venture for me as I became involved in the negotiations with architects, building surveyors and ultimately the builders. As the building went up I attended all site meetings to report back. All went well until one meeting when it came to light that a hole had been cut through one of the main columns to allow an electric cable to come through. It threw the building inspector into a tizzy but they found a way around it. The topping out ceremony was special even attended by the local mayor who named the building ??? The name I can't remember.

Next, it was a site in Surbiton, much closer to home, only four storeys high but the same procedure as for the Croydon project. At the topping out ceremony the local mayor named it Milbank House. The only problem encounted was a local garage that hindered the site. We tried all manner of offers but the owner was intransigent so the architect drew new plans.

The last acquisition I was involved in was the purchase of the Gort Estate. This was a mishmash of sub-standard offices, shops and residences in a large site north of Oxford Street and just off Tottenham Court Road. At one of the planning meetings the architect was explaining how the redevelopment could take place and pointed out an inner ring road to which Lord Girt, in his deep reverberating voice said "it sounds like a jolly good fart to me" causing much mirth. The idea was to redevelop the whole area; there were lots of negotiations with various tenants, which were on going when I resigned

Bernard Pendry

HANNINGTON'S DEPARTMENT STORE

Then a total change of direction: The purchase of Hanningtons, the famous departmental store in Brighton. This meant that Mr. H and Derek spent even less time at Camelford House.

By this point, I was "group accountant" necessitating regular trips to the store, attempting to access the profitability of the various departments. However, they had an internal accountant, not mister lively, but competent so I didn't have much to do but wander round the store meeting all the managers and staff. The store was very reminiscent of 'Are You Being Served' although Mr. H didn't show much likeness to Mr. Grace.

Hanningtons was not your normal purpose built departmental store set out in logical fashion. Quite the contrary: It appeared to have been built up over the years, with different buildings being acquired, some on split levels and other departments in out of store shops. My favourite shop being the men's shop, where I bought a few fashionable clothes.

From having only a handful of staff we now had an army, most of who had been working at the store for many years creating a relaxed working environment.

TIME TO MOVE ON

After nearly 9 years the work presented no challenges, so I decided to seek new employment. I attended a few clandestine interviews, but nothing suited.

During this time a mate at Leatherhead Golf Club, Brian Twyman, had been asking me to join his chartered accountants partnership, Eric Nabarro & Co., I had no intention of going back into the profession but as nothing else presented itself I accepted.

I clearly remember going into Mr. H's office and explaining why I was giving in my notice after nearly 9 years of loyal service. In my wildest dreams I did not expect his reaction: He just nodded, and from that time to the time I left a month later, he never spoke a word to me not even a 'good morning'. Thankfully Derek was entirely different and wished me well as did the charming Mr. Mate. Mr. H's attitude was a pity because I would like to have kept in touch and paid the occasional visit. An earlier incident sums up his character. I was discussing some figures with him when looking out a window I saw a body laying on the Thames riverbank and pointed it out to him. His reaction was we were supposed to be working not looking out of windows.

I had even nominated my successor, Ian Pearson, who easily filled my shoes. During my time there Derek was like the shadow of his father. They went everywhere together and I thought he was never given the chance to break out on his own. I am sure he would have blossomed once he was free of his father's shadow.

THOUGHTS ON MR. H. and DEREK

Derek and I swapped Christmas cards, over the many years right up to his death. On one occasion a few years ago, my wife, Pamela, and I called in at Hanningtons and asked one of the staff to inform Mr. Derek that a blast from the past wanted to say hello. He made us most welcome and invited us to the Brighton Racecourse for the afternoon meeting where he royally entertained us as top steward of the course.

I often wondered how Mr. H became so wealthy. He did say he had owned a farm in Buckinghamshire and, when I joined, not only had he started building his property empire, but also had 2 jewellers shops, one in Aldgate, East London and the other just off Trafalgar Square where I was first interviewed. Apparently in the past he had owned three shops on three of the four corners of the cross roads in Aldgate. Apparently the managers would pass information to each other when customers didn't buy in their particular shop. Every single item was tagged with a specific code of the purchase price, but in code which was DONCASTERX, the D being 1 up to the X being 0. Stocktaking was so laborious and time consuming, with the end results never bearing a significant likeness to the actual stock records.

An advantage of having a watch specialist on the pay roll was when I had purchased a Rolex watch and smuggled it back from Spain in mate Ginge's binocular case, I asked him to check it over. His assessment was that it was definitely not a Rolex possibly equal to a Timex as there were many such watches being made in Ireland. Never bought anything again from a Spanish street vendor.

End note: Derek died in 2010 and Pam & I were invited to his wake held at Brighton Race Course where he had been Course Steward for many years. A splendid affair.

CHAPTER 10

SHEILA and RUXLEY LANE. 1954 to FEB 1968

HOW WE MET

It must have been around 1954 that I chatted up this lovely looking girl at an old school reunion (having both attended Balham & Tooting College of Commerce. BTCC). Sheila was a couple of years younger than me so I suppose I was a bit of a catch (remember in those days I had a full head of hair and was relatively experienced around the fair sex). I took her home and things started to develop but at that time I was also seeing Kathleen Lloyd, Ann Slade, Gillian Wight and any other lucky lady that came along i.e. a typical healthy 18 year old. Also Pat Shadbolt from Colerne was still interested with constant letters and an occasional visit.

Sheila was stunningly beautiful, slim 5'8", gorgeous long legs, long black hair a captivating smile and lips just waiting to be kissed.

However, I did find this one girl relationship a bit daunting and coming home on the 630 trolley bus with Sheila from the Hammersmith Palais after a nights dancing, I dramatically stated that I thought we should cool things off, as I didn't think I was made to be a one-woman man (how dramatic). Now she would normally have stayed on the trolley bus all the way to Earlsfield but on this occasion she was having none of this cooling idea and got off with me for a long chat. And that was me caught hook line and sinker.

MUSHROOM SOUP

A good example of what she was letting herself in for and why she would have been wise to reconsider getting involved was a new milk bar 'Hi Jean' (do they have such things nowadays?) had just opened over Putney Bridge so we gave it a try. On the menu was 'Mushroom soup with stalks' never seen before or since but the idea interested me so that is what I ordered. Up came the soup with not a trace of a stalk. Well I called the waiter over and explained the situation. He politely informed me that sometimes you do get stalks and others you don't. Well I was adamant I wanted some stalks. His demeanour changed from polite to irritation. Off he went and returned with a bowl full of stalks. What could I do but pretend that stalks were the best starter I had ever had. She had been warned.

THE FUTURE IN-LAWS

Soon I was introduced to her parents, Win & Ted Pemble and sister Eileen at their house at 32 Leckford Avenue in Earlsfield SW London, a nice three bedroomed council house that would have been a good buy but Ted did not want to get into a debt with a mortgage. It was on a trip to the coast with Ted, Win and their neighbours that I blotted my copybook. We had trudged over rocks to find a nice secluded spot and while they set about spreading out the blankets and setting up the picnic, Sheila and I went off over the rocks where in a rock pool we found a rather large dead fish. I thought what fun it would be to surprise the others so I picked it up by its tail and from the rocks above threw the fish down like a grenade to where they were sitting expecting howls of laughter. Well it burst open and the smell was horrendous such that we all had to decamp and move further along the beach. I was not very popular.

ALL WORK (AND NOT MUCH PLAY)

At this stage, I was under articles to Jocelyn Miles (chapter 7) and after a full days work and a quick dinner I studied until 9 p.m. then it was usually a walk around to the Durrell Arms for a drink and a game of snooker, so my leisure times were very limited. (Regarding the snooker I am still the reigning champion of the Durrell because as champion in1954 they did away with both snooker tables and turned the room into a lounge). Things developed well with Sheila, we enjoyed dancing, shared the same taste in music and enjoyed each other's company. She was a bit inexperienced on the physical side only ever having one other boyfriend but gradually she became the only girl in my world. Many evenings during my 5 years of study she would come round and in my bedroom read these boring technical books to me e.g. 'Executor Law & Accounts'. I would like to say things developed but there was no lock on the door and Dad had the habit of popping his head in with a cup of tea.

WHISKEY & SODA

Occasionally Sheila would also come round to the Durrell and on one of her first visits I thought I would impress her by ordering a whiskey and soda. Never having drank whiskey I got this idea when doing temporary bar work on a Saturday lunchtime, this local butcher would come in, order a double whiskey add a delicate squeeze of soda, down it before I had rung up the till, order another and as soon as that had gone, so was he. So up came my whiskey and nonchalantly I imitated the butcher and squeezed the soda syphon. Whoosh, in rushed the soda and out rushed my whiskey leaving me with a glass full of soda. Sheila had not seen what had happened so I nonchalantly pretend that was the way to do it while she sipped her Babycham.

THE WEDDING

We married on 23rd May 1959 Sheila 21 and me 23 at St. Mary's Church just north side of the Thames at Putney Bridge (where they filmed The Omen)

The wedding was a wonderful affair with great input by both sets of parents. Sheila looked absolutely stunning in a full length bridal gown offset perfectly by her bridesmaids, Sue (Reg's recently married wife), Eileen and cousin Pauline then a teenager. I wore a smart blue serge suit tailored by Toby of North End Road (A tailor to the Rockers) and winkle picker shoes bought from Russell & Bromley in Bond Street. (They were a little tight and I wore them only occasionally in the future years).

Certainly no society wedding, no dress suits or top hats they were not my scene. No baronial hall for the reception just a council hall, no upmarket caterers just our parents arranged the food. But all in all it was great.

THE HONEYMOON

The honeymoon was in two parts. First night we drove to uncle Len's bungalow in Basinstoke, Hampshire where we enjoyed our first comfortable time together! In the morning there was a knock on the door, quick cover up and there were two guys who engaged me in talks about the bible. Quite interesting but I had other things on my mind so after a few minutes I said, "You sound like those silly Jehovah Witnesses". To my embarrassment, they were.

Then on for a week in Weymouth wandering around the haunts that she had memories of from the many family holidays spent there.

Second honeymoon was in August. I borrowed Dad's fabulous Sunbeam Rapier two-toned black & cream and set off north. I remember pushing the pedal to the metal and attempting to clock up my first 100 m.p.h. along Britain's first motorway, the Preston Bypass (no speeding cameras or CCTV back then! Happy days!) but failed at 98 m.p.h. Before visiting Stewart for a trip around Northumberland we visited Manchester United for their game against Leeds United. The game had only just started when Sheila felt sick and was passed over the heads of the crowd and taken by the medics to a private room with me trailing behind. A few minutes rest, a cup of tea and she was OK, so back to the game! Oh no, we were escorted from the stadium with no refund. This would never have happened at Craven Cottage the home of Fulham Football Club!

OUR FIRST ABODE

Naturally we had been seeking a place to live and in those days buying a property was not even on the cards. We saw some dreadful flats and the best of a bad lot was a first floor flat in Gwalia Street, a side street in Putney S.W. London that I thought was horrendous. However, when we returned from honeymoon Father-in-Law Ted, assisted by Ray, had painted the whole flat including the entrance hall and staircase a bright red. Apparently the old lady who lived down stairs and riddled with arthritis, grabbed hold of the banister rail, as was her want, only to get covered in this red paint. The flat now looked habitable and with the new furniture we purchased, was a good place to start married life. A piece of this new furniture was a Decca stereo record player that coped with records of 78, 45 and 33 r.p.m and is still working but assigned to the garage and only on rare occasions is it used to play my old Hank William's records. (2020 update. It failed to work and is now due for the tip).

SHEILA AT WORK

At this time Sheila was working as a junior secretary at Fortnum & Mason, the upmarket food store in Piccadilly, wealthy customers but Scrooges regarding staff wages so I was pleased when Dad got her a job at the Association of Supervising Electrical Engineers, a love of his life. Better pay but Sheila, not being known for her time keeping, soon blotted her copybook and had to find another job.

Coincidentally at this time I was working with Mr. Lelman, a manager with Jocelyn Miles, who suggested that she should consider going in for modeling and gave me the name of an agency that his wife worked for. Sheila was a most beautiful and elegant lady, tall, slim a cracking pair of legs, wonderful deportment and just gorgeous but would she qualify as a model. She was offered a period of training during which there would be no income so could we afford it? Well we did and she qualified, or whatever models do. Now a much more interesting lifestyle lay ahead for her.

Her first appointments were basic catalogue work, not very exciting but good experience which helped her move on to fashion shows. She looked superb especially in the Chinese chong-sam dresses split to the thigh. This interesting work continued until she fell pregnant so her last engagement was modeling outfits for the expectant mothers.

BIGGER RESIDENCE AND FIRST CHILD

With this new found wealth (she was earning more than me as a qualified Chartered Accountant) on 8th October 1960 we moved to a large 2nd floor flat in Avenue Elmers, Surbiton, large rooms, high ceilings and a great big coal burner in the lounge where I have vivid memories of Sheila bathing baby Mark for the first time, so hesitant with her first child with Win telling her how it should be done. The only downside was the entrance being at the back of the house with a flight of steps having to be negotiated. No problem originally but when Mark came along pushchairs and prams had to be carried.

This was an ideal place for entertaining friends and had some good times playing a variety of games. It was during this time that I joined

Wimbledon Squash & Badminton Club playing most Mondays and Thursdays also joined Leatherhead Golf Club where I partnered John Harris most Saturday mornings.

HOLIDAYS WITH FRIENDS

Before the kids came along most holidays were with friends. Some notable holidays were:

We hired a Dormobile (a 6 seater van) where Archie, Doug, Stewart joined Sheila and me for a camping holiday somewhere in **Cornwall**. We boys slept in a tent while Sheila slept in the vehicle. We had great fun but returning back to camp one night with Archie driving, at the end on this long straight road in the headlights he caught sight of a road ahead but it was a dirt track, the road turning sharp left. He realised the error too late but instead of going down the dirt track he tried to make the left turn, the result being that with screeching wheels the vehicle hit a high earth bank which shot the front wheel right up under the bonnet and we were all propelled forward. Archie had a gash under his chin, Sheila broke a tooth, and Stewart's heel came off his shoe. Doug was first to react and like a real trouper said "This is only a piece of metal thankfully no one is seriously hurt". We couldn't move the vehicle so it was a walk to the nearest village and a taxi to the campsite and in the morning passing the problem over to the hirers.

On a holiday to **Ibiza** we were joined by Archie, Hilary, his friend Don a really nice guy who had this witch, Diane, in tow. No she wasn't that bad but called herself a medium and once got us to join her in an Ouija board session. There we sat extending one finger to rest on the top of an upturned glass surrounded by a circle of the letters of the alphabet while she started intoning 'anyone there' type of thing. Nothing, then the glass started to move and went towards various letters. I tried to work out who was pushing the glass but if anyone was surely the glass would turn, instead it was steady. Diane kept asking questions such as 'who are you' and answers were spelled out with the glass zooming from letter to letter, she was a young girl who had died at the time of the French revolution blah blah. I found it most disturbing and vowed never to engage in any investigation into the occult.

This same holiday we were spending the day in this lovely rocky bay, I was swimming, goggles on, with a lilo by my side when I spied this horrendous creature with tentacles streaming from it, heading straight for me. PANIC, have you ever tried getting onto a lilo when panicking? Well I got on one side; fell off the other when this guy appeared with the creature on his harpoon. I thanked him profusely then realised he had harpooned an octopus and was just swimming into shore.

SON No. 1 (MARK)

As I have said, Sheila was earning more than me so it was a real wrench when she became pregnant but there was no second thought, she would quit modeling and become a mother and housewife. Mark arrived a bouncy baby boy on 9th February 1962 and was the happiest baby ever born. Unfortunately a week old there was a swelling on his eye, the doctor said it would clear up but it got worse and after another two trips to the doctors he decided it needed a specialist examination and arranged a meeting at Moorfields Eye Hospital. By the time of the meeting the eye was quite grotesque and Professor Sawsby diagnosed an abscess and medicated for it. Nothing got better so there were further meetings with the Professor who on further investigations discovered there was a tumour underneath the eye which had pushed it out of its socket, Sheila spent many weeks in hospital with Mark who had to have injections every day and even still he was happy and chuckled all the time but by the time it was brought under control the damage had been done and his vision impaired. The Professor suggested PLAY OPTICS as the only chance of repairing the damage. This entailed a series of lights shone into his damaged eye and having his good eye permanently covered. As you can well imagine it was devastating to watch Mark struggle with this situation and things came to a head when we were due to go on holiday and we could not stand the thought of continuing this treatment, so I phoned the Professor and asked his honest opinion as the chances of this Play Optics working. He said the chances were extremely slim also that the good eye was perfect and should stand him in good stead which was good enough for us and the bandages came off and we had a wonderful holiday.

Mentioning the numerous daily injections they all went OK except for just one, whether the nurse was inexperienced or the needle was blunt he let out a heart-rending yell. A scar developed which is still visible today.

SON NO. 2 (MICHAEL)

Mike was due in June 1966 and because Mark's birth was relatively easy 'they' decided for a home birth. On the day the 18th, I was sent off with Mark while the midwife helped Sheila to deliver. Off we drove to Richmond Park and went for a walk, Mark was full of running but tripped over and went head long into a lake. I dragged him up soaking wet and covered in mud. What could I do now, certainly would not be welcomed at home! Not far away lived aunt Vi so off to her we set being warmly welcomed. Cleaned and dried back to home where we met a tearful Sheila, the birth had been anything but straightforward although the baby was strong and healthy.

A POSSIBLE MISTAKE

Mother-in-Law Win announced that she and Ted would come round every Thursday evening. Sheila raised no objections so neither did I. Presumably they intended baby sitting allowing us to go out. Unfortunately, Thursday evenings were my squash nights so Sheila never got out. Win was a kind hearted person but her bedside manner left a lot to be desired which had a toll on their relationship.

Once I did forgo my squash to get Ted to accompany me to The Green Man Pub where we enjoyed a few drinks and joined in the darts company. I thought this would be the pattern for the future but after a few weeks he declined to come and reverted to his norm of falling asleep in front of the telly waking just in time to go home. I don't know whether this was Win's instruction but I lost a lot of respect for him. What did irk us over the years and later our children, was how Win would go on about Claire and Howard (Eileen and Ray's children) as though they were superior to our three. They remember it to this day.

NEW HOUSE AND MORTGAGE.

In 1965 we thought it was time to buy our own house so we started looking around. The first house of interest was in The Mall, Surbiton, asking price £4,200. Now this was a new game to me so I consulted with Derek Hunnisett, a property man, whose advice was "make them an offer, say £4,000" so I did. Didn't hear anything for a couple of weeks, when I enquired it had been sold at the asking price. A good lesson that I stored for the future.

Next, we were successful in buying 37 The Kingsway, Ewell Village, a two bedroomed bungalow with a lovely garden bordering Glyn Grammar School for the princely sum of £4,400. The move from Avenue Elmers was something else. Brother Reg, Ray, Eileen and Archie came round to give a hand. Thinking that everything would have to be taken out by the rear door, Reg had other ideas. The windowsill of the second floor lounge was nearly 2 feet wide, Reg got out onto the sill and with a strong rope lowered everything bar the heavies like refrigerator down to those waiting below to load onto the vans they had brought round. Great fun.

This was the first place I tried some DIY, not very successfully; the sloping shelves in the new kitchen a good example. The wooden garage was well past its sell by date and leaned at a severe angle, certainly no car would get in. Alongside this garage was a large bamboo pole that presumably had been used when delivering a new carpet and it lay there for years. One day there were a few earwigs scuttling around, I picked up this pole and masses of earwigs fell out so I smashed it and there were thousands. Boiling water did the trick.

We sold Avenue Elmers in January 1968 for £6,700.

BIRTHS & DEATHS

1966 was a sad year for Sheila, in April her father died then in May her granddad, Popsie died. The mood was certainly lightened with the birth of second son Michael Edward Thomas on 18 June.

ONWARDS

Such a lovely bungalow that we thoroughly enjoyed but now with two kids it was too small.

NOW OVER TO LIFE AT RUXLEY LANE.

Bernard Pendry

SHEI & MY WEDDING

NASSAU, CHAPEL
WHERE SHEILA SANG

REG, ME & UNCLLE GEORGE AT HOLIDAY CAMP

LARGE FAMILY CHRISTMAS

MY COUSINS

REG PISSED & MY 40TH

SHEILA IN MODELING DAYS

HOLIDAY CAMP WINNING BEST LEGS

OUR WEDDING

YOUNG NICOLA

CHAPTER 11

2ND PART OF 1ST MARRIAGE

16th February1968 we moved into 30 Ruxley Lane, that is Sheila, Mark age 5, Michael age 2 and me. It cost £9,200 with a mortgage of £8000, a hell of a lot in those days. One of my concerns was Tolworth Station a mile away but Sheila promised to run me there every morning. This promise lasted all of two days.

First big event was Sheila falling pregnant. After the difficult birth of Michael she was taken to Epsom Hospital expecting the birth to be in a few days. On the second day while working in The City of London I got a phone call that birth was imminent so I jumped on my Vespa 150 and did not ease off the throttle until I reached the hospital, parked and sprinted to the ward in time to give Shei a kiss and a cuddle while she was going through the motions. Five minutes later the nurse said, "it's time, let's get to the delivery ward" I didn't think it meant me but she said, "Well are you coming". I had not been present at the birth of our two boys and didn't intend being at this one until the Sister said in a forceful voice "Don't just stand there, let's go" and like a lamb I followed. I positioned myself at the head end whispering coaxing words and it was a bit like you see on the films, pushing, grunting, sweating (and that was just me). There seemed to be lots of activity with coaxing words from the nurses then the cry went up "the baby has arrived". Sheila's first reaction was "is it a boy or a girl" I had a brief glimpse, saw something protruding and said it was another boy. This was soon corrected by the nurse. Apparently all I saw was the umbilical cord.

Now the family was complete with a beautiful little daughter. What should we call her? Sheila decided Nicola but magnanimously allowed me to pick a middle name. At this time there was a pleasant young lady working in the office called Gaye, so that was it. How was I to know that years later the name took on other meanings? This was 9th December 1969.

30 Ruxley Lane is a magnificent house, semi detached but big and solid (people thought it was a Tardis). The kitchen was a major attraction to Shei as it was big with views over the long garden. Also on the ground floor is a substantial lounge with doors opening into the garden, a dining room big enough to get 22 round the extending oak table I had bought some years earlier and an integral garage, never used for a car. Upstairs was 5 bedrooms, Shei & I had the big front bedroom, Nicola a single and Mark and Michael shared the largest bedroom that overlooked the garden, the other rear bedroom kept for guests and the small 5th for different people through the ages. But the major feature is the staircase and landing, the likes of which is rare to find in suburban houses. Big wide L shaped stairs with the landing on all three sides. Over the years this featured in many films with all family and friends congregated thereon and the kids loved climbing over to walk on the wrong side.

Then there was the gigantic attic that stretched the length and breadth of the house. We had it boarded out and installed a 12 feet long scalextric 4 lane track that we all liked competing on. I also had the room partitioned, it had no windows its only use being as a bedroom for the odd occasion, which was only used by nephew Howard when he spent Christmas with us, accompanied by a girl friend. In total darkness they rarely emerged before noon!

But to list a fraction of life during the days at Ruxley is impractical, as it would take volumes. So this is just few things that are worth a mention.

1969 Another major event. In the front garden I spied this very attractive lady tending her front garden just across the road wearing a very brief pair of hot pants, all the latest fashion. Well I had to introduce myself, it was Pam who had just moved into 21 Ruxley Lane with children, David in the same year at Ruxley Lane Comprehensive as Mark so they had a lot in common and Tracy a year older than Michael but they got on like a house on fire and spent hours playing childhood games at one time making a mud concoction to poison Mark and David.

It was not long before Pam and Sheila became good friends. Pam's husband, Mike, soon became known as 'the seldom seen kid' because he worked abroad, rarely came home and when he did he would come in like a whirlwind, mow the lawn and disappear.

Their house backed onto The Old Haileybarians Rugby ground on which after two years of building works The Mid Surrey Squash Club opened. The local kids used the building site as a great play area never mind Health & Safety. Pam, Sheila and I were the first members and this was the start of many years of fun. I had been a regular squash player at Wimbledon so in the early days I was the best player, which only lasted a year or so before the likes of John Harris, and Nick Preece joined. I could write a whole book about the wonderful years as part of this club not just about the squash but notably the card schools followed by trips to Argys, the local Indian restaurant ending at my place for yet more cards which went on to the early hours. Nicola and Michael earned tips serving drinks and Welsh rarebits and in the morning searching for lost coins.

Pam and Mike divorce in 1975 all she got from the divorce was her share of the house sale proceeds, and, to avoid maintenance he arranged for the brewery he was a tenant of to grant Pam a lease of the Hop Bag Pub in Farnhan, Surrey. She knew nothing about running a pub but teamed up with Brian, a Hungarian who had escaped when Russia invaded in 1960. With his help she became an efficient landlady, serving breakfast to as many as 6 guests, getting the pub lively with music and dancing at weekends and getting friendly with the police whose station was just across the road.

They ran this pub until 1981 and this is where I came in again as a knight in shining armour, Brain having run off with one of the young barmaids.

30 Ruxley was the house that saw all the kids and their friends growing up and having lots of fun. Kids birthday parties were something else. The first party was Mark's 9th when he had about 12 friends round. The garden had been left to over grow and the trees on either side had almost met in the middle. I had cut them all back so there was a mountain of branches piled across the lawn and I invented this game whereby on the word go they had to climb over this mountain, touch the walnut tree at the end and get back. Great fun but many cuts and bruises. (See chapter 14)

Bernard Pendry

Other parties that come to mind are Nicola's and on one I had them play murder in the dark; remember her birthday was 9th December. They all had to disperse throughout the house and hide. I would turn off the master switch so no one could turn a light on then start searching the house yelling, "Here comes the bogie man". Lots of screaming and yelling. I don't think it had long-term psychological effects on any of them, but who knows! Then there was jumping down the stairs. I put a mattress at the bottom and in turn they climbed as many stairs as they wanted then jump onto the mattress. The brave got up to about stair 6 but Nicola jumped from stair 7. Game over! But NO, Sara Tallack, a pushy young girl, wanted to do it but I said it was too dangerous. She pleaded and pleaded so in desperation I said she could have one go. Up she climbed, gave a great leap, her head hit the overhead balcony and she came down back first landing heavily on the mattress taking the air out of her making her gasp. The girls thought it was hilarious but it could have been serious. Luckily it wasn't.

The house did have a name '*Longfield*' 125 feet long then enlarged when I bought the end 30 feet of the neighbour's garden making it "L" shaped. Toward the end was a large walnut tree that I built a tree house in about 10 feet up, much later Mike, helped by his mates, built a big two-storey tree house. The supports were long telegraph poles sunk in two feet concrete pits. It will last longer than the house. It got so much use and the side swing could have been lethal. He also dug a pond at the end and then a more substantial one nearer the house with a bridge over. Filling in the old pond there was something wriggling in the mud. On investigation there were a few eels that must have been there for ages as they were caught on a fishing trip to the lakes on Epsom Common. This garden was just great for games, parties and generally having fun. Also ideal for bon fires on Guy Fawkes night when we would have piles of wood mounted by a guy, lots of fire works and a few drinks. One I will always remember is when I made a life size guy and inserted metal poles down both legs, old shoes attached, the poles protruded out the back so by twisting these the shoes moved. It was great looking at their startled expressions when they approached and the guy's feet moved.

We always had fabulous holidays starting with those package holidays to a variety of Mediterranean islands where most of the time was spent in the swimming pools. Later it was more exciting with the pinnacle being the times we spent with Joe Cocker at Hill House, Santa Barbara, the fabulous house he rented from Jane Fonda. These trips quite often coincided with us staying at cousin Bill's in Woodland Hills, Los Angeles. These are times to be savoured.

My diaries are full of my games of golf, snooker, squash, tennis, cards, (3 card brag, hearts which could get out of hand money wise, solo, kalooki, bridge) and lots of fun games.

Shei wanted me to build a cold frame for growing vegetables. Well I prepared an area towards the end of the garden, bought the bricks and cement but I couldn't stop the cement from oozing out of the bricks so I encased them in shuttering. Round three sides I went only to find that the fourth side didn't meet up. I can't remember it ever being used. Another DIY failure.

Being a keen family man I decided that I never saw enough of my cousins, of whom there were many, so I organised a family garden party, everyone was invited including all their children. One stipulation was that everyone had to sport a nametag stating their name and who their parents were. One little boy's nametag read "William, son of gate crasher". He was next-door neighbour's child. It was a great success and we held them many more times.

Shei did like sunbathing and didn't like the white bits. So she would lay on the lounger with cup cakes or whatever over her nipples and even they disappeared (the cup cakes not the nipples). At Wimbledon Tennis fortnight she would open the lounge French door, pull the TV as close to the door as possible, position the lounger just outside and watch the tennis for hours sunbathing naked.

Shei was into Women's League of Health and Beauty to keep her body trim then it was pottery on the wheel I bought her. She made loads of pots and jars but what do you do with the masses of end products once you have made gifts to everyone she knew? Then it was amateur dramatics into which she introduced Mark. Maybe this is where she met Dennis!

Life was good; all the kids were getting on fine then the bombshell. Shei, who had been getting more distant for some time and even Marriage

Guidance sessions didn't have much effect, (the counselor with whom we had many sessions came to the conclusion that Shei had a anti mother complex), announced in July 1980 that she wanted a divorce, she wanted to be Sheila not Bernard's wife. We lingered on for a few months but then she left. I thought at the time that there was no one else but on reflection, Dennis must have been the reason. I soon came to terms with the new situation, me and the three kids doing our own thing, but for the kids sake I wanted their Mum to still be an integral part of their lives so Shei and I agreed she would come back daily to cook for them while I was still at work. I think this worked OK for some years but you never know the long-term effect it may have.

I asked if she would like to work in my office as a typist on a good salary, which she did for a few years until she and Dennis moved to Fleet in Hampshire.

CHAPTER 12

THE RENOIR WINE BAR STORY 1990 T0 1999

Abridged version of the 9 years from 1990 to 1999

1990. A Thursday in July. I get a call from Lou (friend from the early squash club days, who now runs The Red Lion Pub in Horsel near Woking and I am his accountant. We had previously chatted about going into business together). The conversation went something like this:

Lou "We have just missed a great opportunity, a bar in New Malden, Surrey called Chemis came up for sale. I enquired but the owner has already accepted an offer"

Me. "If you think it would be worth buying just give me the owners phone number and I will see what I can do"

Lou. He gave me the guys phone number after saying "It used to be jumping but has been left to run down. However it is in a great position and I know we could bring it back to life"

Me. "Leave it to me".

Next call to the owner:

Me "Hi John, I'm a friend of Lou's and I believe he had been in touch about Chemis"

John "Yes, but I told him it has already been sold and we should be completing next week"

Me "Well supposing we upped the offer by £5,000 and completed next Monday, would you accept?"

John "Tempting but there is no way you could complete in 4 days time, what with solicitors and the landlord with a weekend in the middle".

Me "We do not use solicitors and the landlord will cause no problems. I will draw up a sale/purchase agreement and the money will be there. So what do you say?"

John "If the money is there, you have a deal".

Me "See you Monday"

Now I had to get to work. First thing was to contact Nick Preece (another old friend from squash club days and for whom I acted, and is a successful Estate Agents, Redmans), to ask if was interested, definitely yes, is he always interested in a deal.

The deal was that we put up the money and Lou would make it happen as a 3-way equal partnership. By Monday morning I had our partnership agreement ready to sign, the sale/purchase agreement and the money ready.

NOW IT WAS OURS facing an interesting future.

Lou got to work, plans for a refurb, employed staff (mainly pretty young ladies) most notably SCULLY (a fantastic DJ who was with us all the way through and became a legend playing 60/70s music) and changed the name to RENOIRS.

We opened Friday 16th November 1990. Although our drinks were more expensive than local pubs it took off like a rocket, queues round the block, three doormen making sure there were never more males than females, as Lou insisted this was not going to be a bloke's bar and soon it was jumping to Scully's music. The double door entrance was in the middle, the bar area was in two levels with the DJ consul on the upper level and it was part of Scully's gig to get the upper and lower groups singing against each other creating a fantastic atmosphere.

This was the norm for about 7 years with some ups and downs. Every time we had a special do e.g. Halloween, (Nicola dressed as a headless princess and Carol as The Devil) Valentines Day, were always a sell out and Christmas Eve and New Years Eve were ticket only in those days

£7.50 and £5.00 respectively. Never known so much cash.

One Christmas Eve I had been out with friend Mickey Simmons and about 10 we decided to visit Renoirs. It was rammed full and the doormen were not letting any more in but being the governor OK. The place was heaving, the music was thumping, the singing was loud; all in all a fantastic place to be. What I couldn't understand was why so many had their hands over their glasses then it was explained this was to stop the condensation dripping into their glasses, it was like a rain forest (obviously before the installation of air conditioning). At closing time we left and collected my car from up the road (Only 2 pints all night!). When we approached Renoirs the doors were wide open and it looked as though the place was on fire with a plumb of steam rising into the sky. This was the night that a crowd of them dared me to jump off this table into their arms. Stupidly I did but they were good catchers.

Our big nights were Fridays and Sundays, always packed with regulars, ask son-in-law Neil and his friends. Saturdays were not so good because many Kingston pubs had late licenses, which were a great attraction. We did have a go for a late license but at a meeting came up against a residents committee and you knew from the word GO there was no chance, I just got up and walked out leaving it to Nick.

After a couple of years Scully came up with the idea of opening Christmas nights on the theory that many of our regulars would be bored after a day with Mum, Dad, Nanny, aunt Flo and the like. It worked like magic.

As you will no doubt gather there was lots of CASH about and after a time it dawned on me how unfair it was that the taxman wanted 40% and the VAT man 17% without contributing anything. Well I did take evasive measures but I am not going to own up here.

In 1992 The Red Lion, a large pub/restaurant that Lou had on a long lease, was in need of a major refurb so Nick and I did a deal with Lou, we would put up the money for the refurb and become equal partners in The Red Lion. The cost was about £120,000. This proved to be a rocky road and certainly was not an instant success. It was difficult to keep Lou positive and he didn't agree with anything I suggested e.g. a real ale week, all he could see was the amount of waste but manageress Beverly and I went ahead while Lou took a holiday. If not a roaring profit it was good fun and made many customers happy. Then there was the double sitting for Christmas lunch. Again Lou was against it but decided to go away and leave it to Beverley and me. This was a great profit maker.

Now I recall the parting of the ways.

This set up was fine for a time but Lou became stressed, what with 24/7 looking after The Red Lion and trying to give time to Renoirs he became very negative. We had made various concessions to try to lighten his load but it became clear this was not a healthy situation so in July 1994 we agreed to terminate our partnership and considering the amount Nick & I had spent of the refurbishment Lou owed us £90,000. Later all settled as agreed.

It was also 1992, December 28, Dave Spriggs the cleaner phoned to inform me we had been burgled and the safe was missing, Nick and I were soon down there and met with the police. There was no break-in so obviously it was an inside job. Next day they interviewed Dave, Gary his assistant and Colin the cleaner. Nothing became of this. What really irked us was that the rules were that every night after cashing up the cash would be lodged in the local bank's night safe but on this occasion Dave made the excuse that it was so late he left all the cash in the safe. It had been a very good night and there was over £8,000 in the safe. The safe turned up many week later on open ground with the back oxyocetelened out. Dave didn't stay around very long. I'd still like to know the culprits, rumors abounded but nothing positive. Thankfully our insurers came up trumps.

Close to Renoirs was a Korean Bar and the English manager often popped into Renoirs for one of his many drinks. One day he asked if I would like to see what the Koreans had done to the place. The ground floor was like any other wine bar but the basement was their own playground, lounge chairs all around with a band/dance floor at the end. What amazed me most was along one wall there were shelves containing many bottles of various special whiskeys with tags on each with the name of the owner and how full the bottle was.

Two major problems were the toilet facilities and no air conditioning. We couldn't do a lot about the toilets but after a few years we did install air conditioning. The downside to this was that no longer could the bar staff dance on the bar that had been a feature of the great nights.

Not everything was plain sailing especially stocktaking. It is easy to calculate what stock there should be but ours was always considerably short and the succession of managers we had could never give an explanation. We suspected that a main reason would be bar staff under charging friends but even installing observers nothing ever came to light. Talking of managers, Dave our New Zealand manager had done a good job but in 1994 left to return home and with no alternative we promoted his assistant Martin much to our cost. He had basically been a pot man and had no idea of managing. Sales went down, losses got worse so after many warnings I'd had enough and sacked him with a month's salary. Got a real shock when we got a notice of an Industrial Claim for unfair dismissal. At the Industrial Tribunal he was awarded £7,000 I considered appealing but in our solicitor's opinion we had been lucky as it could have been worse.

Following Chris's departure Scully introduced us to Duncan and Ian with a view to them becoming joint managers. They had a go, changed the name to SUGAR RAYS, spent some money then threw the towel in.

Nick & I took back control and things improved a bit but it was clear that the deal with Scully was not sustainable so I put a new deal to him. His basic wage would be reduced but replaced by a bonus if weekly sales exceeded £6,000 to start in 1996. He protested that he couldn't survive on less money. No option other than to give it a try. Well I don't know what he did but sales rocketed and he had never earned so much. Wonderful what a carrot can do.

Unfortunately our time at top of the tree ended and trade dropped off prompting us to put it up for sale. I thought it would be an ideal buy for either an individual or a group because we were not beholden to any supplier, we appointed Savills, no rush and the only offer was from a local Korean family who wanted to open it as a Noodle Bar. So now time to have a party.

It must have been Scully who got the word around that RENOIRS was closing because on Sunday 29th August 1999 I arrived there at 5.10 to witness a queue going down the High Street under the railway bridge and the 5 doormen on duty were keeping the line in order. As I have said, we tried for a late license without success, so Scully decided we should open at 5.30.

I had decided that all drinks would be £2.50 (no doubles). Daughter Nicola was on the top bar with Gary, five lovely ladies were on main bar and when the place got so packed we opened the rear door that led onto next door's car park putting two more staff in charge with a Bud only bar and soon this also was crowded. Put it this way, the two staff manning the rear door never asked for any wages. I had lain on more supplies than ever before but soon it was clear we needed more, first it was £100 worth of bottles from the bar next door, then I phoned Nick who had not yet arrived and asked him to call into every off-licence on his way and buy up whatever. I drove round to mate Keith's pub, The Castle, and bought whatever he could spare. The night was a joyous riot a fantastic carnival night; just ask Son-in-Law Neil and his mates who were there. We ran out of wine glasses so had to use pint glasses. The takings were phenomenal.

After customers were gone only Scully and the doormen, (four black and one white) were left. The head burly doorman challenged their wages saying Scully had agreed they should get three times normal rather than the double I was prepared to pay them. Scully said he had never discussed wages. They became quite threatening and although it could have been a dodgy situation I stood my ground in the faith that they would not cause trouble because it would mean them losing their license.

What a mess in the morning and many souvenirs, banister rails, posters etc. gone.

An end to a most enlightening and enjoyable period.

CHAPTER 13

SHEILA GONE - PRE PAM

1980 had been a tumultuous year, failing to patch up our marriage with Sheila and I amicably agreeing for her to move out leaving me with the three children. In the November Sue had moved in as my girlfriend so there was now five of us soon increased when first Jake (really Jacqueline), Mark's girlfriend, then Nicola's school friend Sara moving in. Both had left behind troubled home life. Michael just had a succession of girl friends.

Now it was like a Kibbutz, me the head Honcho, Sue doing most of the cooking, Jake being the foreman giving the rest various jobs.

An early purchase was a very sturdy pool table that dovetailed as our dining table. This got a lot of use especially by Michael and his school friends so he got to know every nuance and rarely ever lost. (After all these years I still have the table tucked away and pool never played).

Then, after some practice on the dry ski slopes at Sandown Park, there were the skiing holidays the first holiday was to Flaine, just the three kids and me. What a fabulous holiday we had, more bonding than ever before and such laughs especially at a dinner one night when the fish I had ordered came up looking like a monster. It may have been the same evening when, after dinner at a restaurant a little way up a slope, I got a little inebriated and stumbling down a slope in deep snow but they all took good care of me.

 The next skiing holiday was to Kitzbul including Sue and Jake. Kitsbul is not just for skiing, as it is a beautiful Austrian town with fine shops and plenty of eateries. At one restaurant where we regularly visited we became very friendly with the manager and one evening he treated us to a house specialty, a light paste on toast. Delicious but he shouldn't have then told us it was deer's brains.

Mark having left school and got a job with Matthew Hall a construction company based just south of London Bridge and to save money he cycled there every day. This lasted a few years getting nowhere ignoring advice given by friends who knew the company, informing him of the person to contact to get promotion. He did nothing so in desperation to get him out of this malaise I suggested he come to work for me when he could take whatever time he needed to attend interviews. He never attempted to look for another job but he learnt bookkeeping and became a valued employee. Years later I got him a bookkeeping job with tenants of mine, Barrelfield Limited who ran a property advertising paper. He did invest in their shares, which turned out a good investment when they sold out. He married Jake, had two super boys, Matthew & David, amicably divorced then married Steph, in those days like a wispy nymph, living happily ever after.

As a late teenager he formed a rock band, "Rhythmic Itch". They used our huge loft for practice and what a racket it made being heard streets away.

Michael left school with no idea what to do and a litany of jobs followed, a week for an engineering company drilling holes, didn't impress, worked for Michael Holloway in some travel company in the West End, didn't like the travel so moved to a local travel firm selling holidays, then off to a graphic designers in Godalming in Surrey travelling daily on his small Harley Davidson, a stint in Sainsbury's butchery department where he learnt how to dissect a carcass and finally a year at The La Manga Resort, Spain, helping out in the pro shop and organizing tournaments. Back in England he worked temporarily for a friend, Barry Steel, in the tree game. He took to this like a duck to water, set up his own business M & M Tree Surgeons Limited and later M & M Gardens.

Only last year he sold the well appointed family house in Surrey and bought a 360 years old thatched cottage in Meonstoke, a small village in the west of Hampshire with the intension of renovating it back to its original state while living in a large caravan on the site. A major project. Wife Nicki, daughter Olivia and son Charlie were skeptical but soon came round to enjoying village life.

Nicola fell in love with horses and with friend Sara spent every spare moment at Keith Tollick's stables shoveling shit with an occasional ride. One day she came to me "Dad I hope you won't be cross but I have taken £500 out of my bank account and bought a lovely horse called Tufty" She told me the story of how they were to get rid of him so I told her how thrilled I was for her. A year or two later an American lady was returning home and asked Nicola if she would like her horse 'Dandy'. A powerful mount that Nicola fell in love with and told stories of the excitement of galloping with him. Husband Neil wasn't too pleased with the costs! As an aside she played netball becoming team captain.

Sue after two gloriously happy years decided she wanted children. As I had already had three plus also having had the 'chop' it was a none starter for me. We had long discussions but amicably we parted. She ended up marrying Peter Osborne one of my managers.

1983 camping holiday in France. First night after erecting the tent, borrowed from June Conboy, we went out to dine, I had a couple of wines but when we came out the heavens had opened and there was a massive deluge. In pitch darkness we got into my new Ford XR4i, found the road but the windscreen wipers had difficulty in clearing the rain, so gingerly I started down the road. All of a sudden the car lurched to the left and stopped at a worrying angle. Mark offered to get out but not knowing what dangers there might be (could be on the edge of a cliff), I told him to stay and gingerly slowly inch-by-inch the car got back on the road. The scene that met us back at the campsite was horrendous, the tent had collapsed, the contents soaking and surrounded by French fellow campers. What had happened is that I had not used the guy ropes so the weight of the water was too heavy for the tent poles to bear. What could be done? The French were marvelous, they lent us five sleeping bags, a two-man tent for Mike and me, another let Nicola sleep with their daughter and Jake and Mark let down the seats and slept in the car. The scene in the morning, many tent poles bent and twisted, every bit of clothing sodden, as was the map book. Fortunately the sun shone so everything dried by noon. We did have to put splints on many of the tent poles.

A few days later we pitch the repaired tent right on the banks of a tributary of the river Loire, quite idyllic. Lovely day sun bathing and swimming so all was well until we turned in for the night. Then there was an eerie feeling, everything went deadly quiet, and then a wind started gaining force. Aware of what had happened previously, Jake, Nicola, Mark and I held on to the tent poles while Michael was outside trying to hammer in the tent pegs as the gale turned into a hurricane that raged for about 30 minutes before it subsided to nothing. In the morning there was devastation around us, caravans were turned over and one right in the river. Apparently this hurricane had affected the whole area practically destroying the nearby seaside town.

It was on this holiday while canoeing that Mark demonstrated the technique he had learnt at Sea Scouts of the Texas role. Over he went, seconds passed, no sign of Mark, and then he emerged spluttering. Apparently you are supposed to have a cover preventing the water from entering the canoe.

CHAPTER 14

IN COMES PAM

In December 1983 out of the blue Pam Holloway, an ex neighbour and friend, phoned to ask if I would give her a reference because after years of running The Hop Bag Pub in Farnhan, her partner Brian had gone off with one of the bar maids and she was selling up and hoping to go back to work at The Ministry of Defense. Of course, no problem however it coincided with me needing a partner to go to one of my clients Christmas lunches at the best restaurant in Cobham, Surrey, La Capana. Who was to know this was the start of 30 years of happiness! First I dealt with her tax problems for which she treated me to a weekend away at a spa hotel where she prepared a bubble bath for me but must have put in a double dose because bubbles became a mountain escaping into the bedroom.

After she sold the pub her and son David bought a house in Blackwater so courtship was a bit spread out. A few years later they put the house on the market, the first enquirer's surveyor pointed out there was subsidence. Great consternation as many insurance policies exclude such damage, thankfully it was covered by their insurance policy. It didn't delay the selling of the house, as soon as it did sell Pam moved closer to Chessington and it was not long after that that she moved in with me.

So THE FAMILY was extended to include not only Pam but also her children, Tracy and David not forgetting Sherry the Springer Spaniel, not liked by many.

Grandkids come along year after year Lucie 1988, Matt 1990, Ed 1991, David and Lara 1992, Mollie and Taylor1995, Georgia and Charlie 1997, Olivia 1998 then long wait, Tess 2005, Harvey 2008 finally Cali 2011.

No more on the scene now so waiting for great grandchildren! Matt is living with Alicja, David living with Louise, both planning weddings for

Bernard Pendry

2021 (they had planned 2020 but lockdown rules prevented this), Mollie courting Jack, Charlie courting Sophie. When will someone produce a great grandchild? Not Lara, the first in the family to 'come out'.

On holiday at the Dona Lola complex in Calahonda southern Spain we were accosted by time-share girls and did fall for their invite. The project being sold seemed OK and it was suggested I should sign up there and then. I said I wanted to study the contract, to be told it wasn't done that way. At that stage I lost my cool, called all the other prospective buyers to attention and gave them the advice not to sign until they had run the contract by their legal representatives. It did not go down well with the time-share people. Departing Pam insisted on getting the promised bottle of champagne.

Anyway, back at the resort someone pointed out the for sale sign in the next block so I visited the agents offices to show my interest. They told me it was up for sale at 50,000 euros and that the owner was not prepared to accept less. Anyway I visited the resort's offices and while waiting for the receptionist to get off the phone, got chatting to a Mr. Alan James who asked if I would be interest buying his beach house. He took me to inspect his property and it was the one I had already enquired about. The place was lovely so I asked the price, 40,000 pesetas and we shook hands. Unfortunately because I had already contacted the selling agents he was hesitant because now agent's fees had to be paid. Thinking quickly I said "No worry as I will be buying the property in my partners name, Pamela Holloway". (This didn't turn out to be a wise move because later it caused many problems). The deal went ahead surprisingly easy, we both shared the same bank, the notary asked a few questions, and money changed hands, deal done.

This was to be our family holiday home for many years. Such wonderful times were had especially for Pam and I who spent three months in the winter there with her dog Sherry.

When Pam died it past to our five children, a lot of money was spent modernizing it and was rented out for a couple of years which gave so many tax problems when Spain changed its tax laws prompting the children to sell it for 300,000 euros.

Pam had divorced Mike in September 1975 and we married on 8th May 1999. I really did see this life being ours forever, lots of fun, holidays, safaris, cruises, lots of socializing with family and friends. We were living at 30 Ruxley Lane when developers suggested they maybe interested in combining it with an adjacent property in a development and suggested an option to buy. This came to nothing but it did make us have a look around. Any move would have to be very special. We toured around and driving into a recent development of one of the five mental hospitals built in the early 1900s at the orders of Queen Victoria in order to get the mentally ill out of central London, now called Clarendon Park, Epsom, there was a for sale sign with the house tucked around a corner, hardly visible. What a magic location, so secluded and when we met the owners we agreed to buy at the full asking price £545,000. The sellers were a couple that were divorcing and Pam just hoped they would not make up. First thing we did was to get son Mike to put a gate in the side fence opening onto the nature reserve and a path down to the local Horton Golf Club.

Thinking this would me our house forever I bought it in our joint names. As it turned out, do I have regrets?

Life was good, many holidays, garden parties, always interacting with family and grandchildren.

Then another bombshell, Pam contracted the big C and after a three year struggle past away on 14th July 2013. Shattered I am now a bachelor once again. (Chapter 21).

OLD CHUMS GROUP

PAM & THE PALACE

PAM & ELEPHANTS

EARLY CRUISE

The Story Keeper : A Memoir of Love and Survival

PAM WITH BLACKPOOL TOWER IN BACKGROUND

DUBAI & THE MOUNTAINOUS SAND DUNES

PAM CAR CRASH

CHAPTER 15

THE WIDOWER FINDS TRUE LOVE

I am devastated by the loss of Pam so thinking it is a bachelor's life for me. So what can I do?

SINGING? Thought singing would be fun so in May joined The Epsom Male Voice Choir ready to do a bit of singing. It was nothing like I thought it would be, not just a singsong but also so pernickety that I really didn't have a clue. Everyone was encouraging, it was clear they all knew music; most had been choristers for many years whereas my singing was limited to the bathroom. So I sat at the back doing my pathetic best. However I did get a moment of fame. They were rehearsing songs for a First World War show, one of the songs the name of which escapes me, but the men were in the trenches with shells coming over and everyone had to go "whizz-bang". I let out my loud whistle which was more realistic and the conductor immediately said "your in". Unfortunately I had already decided to quit.

LEARNING THE PIANO? Isn't this something everyone dreams of? Well in October I bought a Roland F-20 electronic keyboard and signed up for lessons with a local lady. She tried hard, scales, middle C, Clefts, quavers, tempo, rhythm: I gave it a go with weekly lessons but nothing sank in so after a few months it became blatantly obvious I didn't have what it takes. Did attempt to play some Christmas carols to the family, which caused great laughter when they couldn't recognize any of them.

CROQUET

Rosemary Ackerman, a lady I occasionally played bridge with at The Royal Automobile Club introduced me to the game of croquet at The

Surbiton Croquet Club. Having no previous idea of the game I found it interesting and soon joined the club and henceforth played every week. As my golf deteriorates my skills at croquet blossoms.

OTHER TIME CONSUMERS.

Lots of interaction with the family:

Took granddaughters Lara and Mollie to lunch at the RAC.

Went to see thespian Mark in "Death Trap"

Tracy discusses her credit card problems. I paid them all off getting fully repaid over a short period.

Took Nicola & Tess to Chessington World of Adventure

Use Steph & Mark's birthday present to take Nicola to The Shard, the tallest building in the U.K., followed by lunch in Borough Market. Thoroughly recommended.

Took all the family plus dogs to the log cabins at Dorset Hotel and Country Club. Attractive Swedish Log cabins, three en suit bedrooms and huge lounge perfect for a self-catering holiday.

Took all the family to a Fancy Dress Dinner Dance at the RAC Club

Held a garden party for family including cousins

Joined Nicola and family in Nerja, Spain for holiday

Bought Tess a new bigger bike.

Golf holiday with Mike, Pete, Nick Preece at Macarena C.

Major events of the year:

Malaysian airlines disappears over the China Sea with 227 passengers

This was never recovered.

Start writing the Joe Cocker book. Chapter22.

Rolf Harris found guilty as a paedophile.

Injured Grandson Taylor goes to a lovely new home in Sunbury.

Scottish referendum. Yes 45 to 54 to stay.

12th November Dad dies age 81.

Cousin David Fox dies.

New Bosch electric bike £1899. Allowing me to keep up with the kids

Bernard Pendry

MY BACHELOR DAYS COME TO AN END

On 23ʳᵈ December 2014 I invite Sue to join me for lunch not having seen her since 1982. This is our story.

THE WONDER OF SUE OR TRUE LOVE

I first met Sue when, as a 16 years old she came to work at Eric Nabarro & Partners, as an office junior. She progressed and became my secretary at our offices in Great Marlborough Street, London. Having got fed up with commuting in 1980 I bought an office in Surbiton, 124 Ewell Road, intending to move my section there. A couple of the staff, including Sue, helped with the move and at the end of the day Sue's brother was supposed to collect her and take her back home in Kent. However he called off so she was faced with an arduous journey. I suggested she might like to stay with the kids and me and go home in the morning. She was thankful and that evening she accompanied me to a friend's party. There was quite a lot of drinking and Sue had her fair share. Back home I showed her into the spare bedroom and an innocent goodnight kiss started off two years of a lovely romance that soon my three kids accepted. Wonderful years.

However, her bodily clock started ticking and she wanted children. Friendly discussions followed the result being there was no way we could stay together because I already had three children also had the chop so we had to say goodbye. I missed her so much, my heart was bleeding and my gut wrench when I found out she had teamed up with Peter Osborne my manager. I thoroughly understood her reasoning and with no recriminations wrote her an emotional loving letter, which included a line, 'maybe sometime in the future fate will be kind enough to bring us together.' So farewell.

33 years passed.

Being a bachelor with time on my hands I started writing a book about my years befriending Joe Cocker, the Rock & Roll singer, and sought the memories of various people who had been around in those years would enhance the book. One was Sue. The only way to contact her was via her husband whose phone number I acquired from a mutual friend. I invited her to lunch at the RAC Club in Epsom on 23rd December 2014.

The lunch was much reminiscing but with no mention of our past love. She came home for coffee and more friendly reminiscing but nothing further. Just as she was getting into her car we kissed goodbye. Well it was like a THUNDER CLAP. We went our separate ways but the damage was done, we had to see more of each other. Tough days followed, especially for Sue who was married and mother for three adult boys. Of course we had long chats trying to make sense of the situation but it soon became clear we had to be together so on 21st January, just 30 days later, she moved in. Immediately we were back in love but she had to weather some hard times and go through mediation, which we survived and were married exactly two years later on 21st January 2017. She presented me with a framed note '23rd December 2014 The Day we fell in love AGAIN'.. It sits in pride of place in my study. All the extended family welcomed her with open arms.

Sue had spent the past 30 years as housewife, chauffeur, mother and odd job person. She seemed pretty bored with not a lot going for her. This soon changed, I introduced her to croquet and in the first year she won 2 trophies, became my equal at table tennis (although that doesn't say too much), matured from pool to snooker, got into cycling with me, started playing a myriad of board games and exuded happiness and enjoyed being in love, much reciprocated.

I could ramble on for ages, just be assured life is fantastic.

Bernard Pendry

SCHOOL CHUMS AT OUR WEDDING

SUE & MY WEDDING

CHAPTER 16

THE NABARRO ERA 1970/1990

Mega thanks to Brian Twyman, a friend at Leatherhead Golf Club, who gave me the opportunity to escape from the Hunnisetts and join with him and his partners in Eric Nabarro & Co. Chartered Accountants. They had two offices, one in London, and one in Putney High Street that was run by partner Richard Atkins.

The primary reason they wanted me was to look after their client, Nigel Thomas, a manager in the music industry. At the time he had a few nondescript artistes and to me he was spending more promoting them than the royalties received. But soon on he managed to get Joe Cocker under contract and then my life altered dramatically. I won't go on as it is covered in chapter 22.

The London offices occupied the whole building of 11 Great James's Street in Holborn just west of the City of London and were rented from Hazlemere Estates Limited. Having spent 9 years at a property company I enquired why they didn't buy the freehold to be told they had tried but Hazlemere were not interested. About this time I was enquiring about buying the chartered accountancy business, Leslie A. Ward & Partners who occupied two floors at 3/4 Great Marlborough Street in the West End. I was not yet a partner but put a deal to them: (a) If I could organise for us to buy the freehold and sell it in on for a profit and (b) buy the Leslie A Ward practice and (c) move their practice into the Ward offices would I be entitled to 20% of the profit made to the property deal. They agreed.

I contacted Hazlemere and at first got a total 'not interested in selling' response to which I said, "everything is for sale, it just depends on the price". He went away to think about it. In the meantime I contacted

Bernard Pendry

local commercial estate agents to enquire what the property would be worth, vacant. The result was that on the same day we bought and sold the freehold, making £75,000 profit, purchased Leslie A. Ward & Partners from Norman Wood, and moved into their offices at 3/4 Great Marlborough Street where we remained. After this I became a partner.

The partners were an odd bunch. Eric Nabarro, the founder, was a devout Jew but during my time he never attracted any new clients. The only thing I learnt from him was taking something to read when going to the loo, his favourite was the Taxation magazine. When he was a sole practitioner he made Kanti Shar a partner even though he was not qualified. Kanti was a good worker and ran a profitable section but never had any ideas of expanding the practice. Next he took on Brian Twyman, a pedantic fellow with big ideas hence his taking me on. His forthright approach was quite dominating and he seemed to get his own way on most things. Then there was Richard Atkins, quite the eccentric genius type, very clever especially regarding tax but some of his ideas were off the wall. He worked odd hours e.g. getting into the office gone midday then working to midnight. When we moved out of Great James's Street he set up offices in Putney, south London where he remained for many years, well past his 70th birthday.

After about a year I suggested we should have a meeting to set out plans for the next 5 years. Good idea and a meeting was arranged at The Talbot Inn, Ripley, Surrey. Eric, Kanti, Richard and I were all seated waiting for Brian. In he strode and without even sitting down, gave us an ultimatum, he wanted to be managing partner with limited client contact and would drive the practice forward and left us to think it over and off he went. Well we sat there dumbfounded wondering what planet he was from. Needless to say we parted company soon after.

The most sole destroying part of being a practicing accountant, or any professional for that matter, it has only one asset and that is time. This necessitated keeping records of every minute, the dreaded time sheets. I could be in the office by 8.30 a.m. not leaving until 7.30 p.m. with no lunch hour and still only account for 6 hours out of the 11. Then when you get the print outs telling you how much should be invoiced to clients there are always disbeliefs as to how so much time could have been spent.

So you take a deep breath and send the invoice. (This time awareness followed me after retirement and even now I am conscious of time).

I was the only partner who tried to expand the business. As well as negotiating the purchase of Leslie A. Ward and taking on Norman James the senior partner, I negotiated buying Lenton & Co taking on Norman Wood as a manager, Thompson Levett & Co taking on Dick Levett as manager, later as a partner. They were all reasonably successful.

There was a peculiar incident with Norman James. One day Ralph Leach, a brilliant manager who basically ran the office, came into my office to tell me that Norman was acting very strangely and thought I should do something. So I called Norman in, sat him down and asked him to tell me what was wrong. He sat there as in a trance and kept staring out of the window. With some prompting, mournfully he said "I've done something bad" and went silent. After a lot more prompting it turned out that it was something to do with one of his client's tax return. What it was he didn't seem to remember and he just sat staring over the rooftops. Then he said, "They are out to get me" "who" I asked "Them over there" he said pointing to some workmen way in the distance. This had taken over an hour so I called in Colin Haffenden, a senior clerk and asked him to take Norman by taxi to Waterloo Station and see him onto a train to Uckfield where he lived. Off they went and Colin returned some time later. I asked if it had gone OK, he said "When I turned round after paying the taxi driver Norman had disappeared and I couldn't find him". Later I phoned his wife to enquire if he had arrived home. She seemed unconcerned displaying no sympathy and off hand said "Yes he got home eventually". It wasn't many weeks later that he committed suicide by throwing himself off a train. Very sad.

I had other ideas for expansion, opened an office in Heathfield, East Sussex as many of the Leslie A. Ward clients were in that part of the world. At first the office was in a first floor office above Errey's Furniture store, a client, and I employed loveable Jack Beard who got on so well with the locals. Later I set up a mini partnership with Rosie Hotham, a local chartered accountant, took an office in the high street and expected good things. Unfortunately it did not work out so I dropped out and left it to her. Many years later I was served a judgment summons of £12,000 for unpaid rent, me being joint lessee. Of course we paid up but try as I might I never did get a penny from her or her husband who was joint tenant. Another lesson learnt.

Next, somehow I got in touch with David Terry, another chartered accountant, who knew there was a practice for sale in Haywards Heath, Sussex and enquired if we would go into partnership and buy the practice. He seemed an honest fellow well presented, and the practice had some good clients, so we invested on the understanding that he would be the local partner and be responsible for running the business. Nice offices, good staff, what could go wrong? Our policy was that clients should be billed quarterly depending on work done. Other accountants only billed on completion of a project e.g. finalisation of accounts. Things seemed to be going OK but cash flow didn't meet up with work invoiced. While David was on holiday stalwart Ralph Leach and I went down for an investigation. Behind a filing cabinet we discovered a mountain of invoices never sent. We took over and righted the ship but the damage was done and we wanted out so it was put on the market for sale.

I entered negotiations with Mr. Howley, another chartered accountant who was interested in buying a 75% interest with David Terry remaining as a 25% partner. He conducted a full diligence investigation and the deal went through. Most of the money was paid but he still owed £5,000, which was to be paid in 3 months time. Well nearly a year went by and no payment, so I instituted legal proceedings, there was no defense so a judgement summons was issued. When further action was taken to recover the balance he registered a defense with the High Court irrespective of the time that had passed, and they agreed for a meeting to discuss his defense. At the High Court hearing I pointed out to the judge (a very pleasant individual) that the defense was absurd trying to compare the value of work-in-progress at the time of purchase to a year later. I explained to the judge that work-in-progress was a moving thing and varied daily, therefore to try to compare the value at different dates was absurd. I don't think the judge truly understood what work-in-progress is. I also put forward the theory Howley had come up with this ruse to delay making the payment. The judge seemed bemused but decided to give Howley time to prepare his defense provided the outstanding money was paid into court. This he did and the case just dragged on even though my lawyers pointed out to his solicitor and council the flaws in his defense, I was confident of winning and that he would have to pay not only his lawyer and counsel but also mine. This didn't seem to have much effect and it wound on to a full trial at the High Court. The day before his legal team wanted to do a deal but I was so confident, I flatly refused any compromise.

Without going to court they capitulated landing Howley with a huge debt. I not only got the £5,000 but interest from day one and all my costs. In retrospect it brought into question the honesty of the legal profession, how could not only his solicitor but also his counsel have led him to believe he had a leg to stand on!!!!

Our clients were pretty run of the mill, accounts, tax, and some financial advice: not very exciting. Some worth a mention:

The Miles families. They had been traditional cattle farmers for many years as had their parents based in West Sussex owning about 800 acres plus an abattoir and shop. John the elder brother was the main man and ran every administrative side of the business while brother Jim was in charge of the cattle. When I first started to act for them they were traditional farmers who had little or no interest in anything else. They were a jovial couple and I got on with them very well. In time I got them out to expensive restaurants and opened their eyes to other possibilities, the best one being when they went to The Calgary Stampede in Canada. Early on I visited Jim at Rickney Farm with son Mike, as he was out his wife, April, showed us round the place and in a barn there were a few empty pig stys. Their Jack Russell terrier jumped into one of the stys and was in an agitated state rushing around. April said he must have the scent of a rat that must have been in there sometime. There was a length of drainpipe laying down one side and she said "Mike just pick that up". He did so and out ran this huge black rat. I don't know who moved faster, Mike who jumped in the air or the rat, but fastest of all was the terrier that in a split second had broken the rat's neck. Mike had a quick change of underwear! Another time Jim took us what he called *'lookering'* driving round in his truck to see that the cattle in the myriad of fields were OK. In one field he asked Mike to carry a bale of hay into the middle. The cattle were in the far side but when Jim sounded his cow horn cattle from miles away started running towards us. Well Mike was in their path and they ran faster than him so he threw himself into a hedge. Great mirth.

Everytime I visited I had meat orders from the wife and friends to buy from their shop. It was always superb meat and although they offered me some deals I always said "I'll pay for the meat you just pay my bills". Things were going great until 9th January 1978 when at a partners meeting I had a phone call from Jack Beard to inform me that John had died. A great shock. I knew he was a big red meat eater and was over weight but didn't see this coming, as he was only 49. I attended his funeral at the local church but never wanting to go close to any grave I was standing back when on a hill in the back ground I saw John standing there with a big smile on his face. Never had such an experience before or since.

Now what would happen to the business as now there was only the cattle minder, most of us thought Jim would not be able to cope. How wrong we were, it is amazing what the human spirit can do when the need arises. Jim, who had always been in the background, took over as though he was made for it and the business didn't suffer at all. Shortly after there was a government ruling that all abattoirs had to conform to new rules if they wanted to continue trading. There were huge grants available but the hoops one had to jump through were tortuous and we spent masses of hours conforming. In the long run it was worthwhile and they had a brand new abattoir.

Jim had a new girlfriend Sandra, and wanted a divorce. His three children, Robbie, Yvonne and Helen were of course upset but divorce happened and he married Sandra with whom he had a kiddie. Things seemed to settle down but not many years later he died, reputedly on 'the job'. Now things really hit the fan. I was his sole executor and in his will the main beneficiary was Sandra and provisions for his three children. I don't know what had been in brother John's will but the business was still dealt with as 50/50 with John's son, David taking his place. Being executor I had to investigate all Jim's finances before I could obtain Probate in the course of which Robbie produced a key that he thought was for a security box at the bank. Armed with the key I met with the bank manager who explained that I was entitled to inspect the two boxes but as I had not yet obtained probate he would have to be present. When the boxes were opened all I saw were tax problems, there was £82,000 in five pound notes. (Imagine if I had already acquired probate, the cash could have just disappeared!) Obviously he had been creaming off cash from the business. What could I do? Well as the last accounts of the business had not been sent to the Inland Revenue I included the money as takings also 50% was presumably owed to brother John's family. Another result was ex wife, April, came out fighting because she had contended all through the divorce that Jim had hidden cash. The courts awarded her £60,000. Robbie and Yvonne thought they were entitled to more and instructed independent solicitors to investigate, hinting that I had not acted properly. (As if!). The end result was nothing changed; they had legal costs while Helen the youngest, who had no gripe with me, received her full entitlement. The business continued to be run by the two sons, David and Robbie.

Redman & Co. This was an estate agency business started by my great friend Nick Preece and his partner Peter Gurd who had both been salaried partners in Ellis Copp Estate Agents. What a gamble. They opened with one office in New Malden, Surrey but it didn't take long before they started to expand with more offices and more partners, Mike Honour and Richard Jackman. Nick and I worked closely together always doing cash flow forecasts that never came out remotely accurate but still the business expanded in leaps and bounds. Then came that crazy period when financial institutions, namely building societies, thought estate agents were an avenue into fortunes to be made selling mortgages and of course Redmans were approached by several institutions. All these people were only interested in the figures so Nick and I produced reams of reports setting out how professional and prosperous the business was and the planned expansion plans for the future. We attended many meetings with directors and their legal aids all were keen to do a deal. Most of them wanted the price to be dependant upon future profits but Nick, being a wise old bird, took the line "that once you take over you will want things done your way so whatever deal we do will be a once and for all deal". It worked, and General Accident went ahead making the partners wealthy. What nobody saw coming was the crash in the property market that happened only months after the sale and all those institutions lost many millions. Nick stayed, as an employee for a year then was free as a bird. He has an occasional nightmare thinking what would have happened had they not sold, bankruptcy possibly.

Mott Green & Wall (MGW). Derek Mott was another friend from Mid Surrey Squash Club whose business along with his partners was as unqualified surveyors in the commercial property market and was very profitable. Derek knew of the part I played in the sale of Redmans and asked if I would like to get involved in either raising capital for their business or finding someone to buy the business. I told them what was involved and we came to an agreement that if I found a buyer for the price that was acceptable to them then my fee would be 1% of the sale price if after all this work it came to nothing there would be no fee. During the negotiations leading up to the sale of Redmans I had meetings with the directors of a company Abaco who seemed interested in buying any business that was making profits with the idea of forming a conglomerate to launch on the stock exchange. Well the sale of MGW went like a dream for many millions (I still have a copy of the cheque for £7,792,012) and the final signings took place in the famous George the V in Paris. A great result until I rendered my invoice then there was silence. When I pressed the point suddenly my "friend" Derek was not to be contacted and Peter Green took over. He said he had no knowledge of the agreement that Derek had made and proposed a settlement of £50,000 way below what I was due. Of course I discussed the situation with our solicitors whose advice was "although you confirmed in writing the agreement you had made with Derek, whether on purpose or not, they did not send an acknowledgement. Now you are up against partners who are recent millionaires and Derek is legalistic, you should consider accepting their offer because a legal battle would be costly and could go either way so my advice is accept the offer". We took his advice and I just lamented how sad it is that you can't trust friends.

There was a sequel to this episode. The partners of MGW took their millions in shares in Abaco who, a little while later, were taken over by British & Commonwealth Ltd swopping their shares for B & C share. It was not many years later the British & Commonwealth went into liquidation, the shareholders getting nothing. I believe that both Green & Wall had sold their shares but Derek hung on. Tragic!

ERREYS was owned by three brothers, Derek, Colin and Hugh Saunders based in Heathfield, Sussex. Derek ran Erreys Furniture Store in the High Street, Colin ran the printing works, both reasonably successful and Hugh tried to look after the accounts thankfully aided by an internal accountant. I used to visit them every month to discuss the management accounts and give advice whenever needed. It became clear that Hugh was struggling and certainly not enjoying his work. So one day I took him to lunch for a friendly chat and discuss his situation not just at work but his life in general. It was clear he had no money worries so I suggested that he should call it a day, retire and do the things he liked. He took my advice and never looked back. I gave Robert Harris, a director of Arcolectric, similar advice with the same result; he just enjoyed various hobbies without the worry of business.

Of course there were many other clients but none that I got personally involved with to any extent.

What a way to be conned and lose money!

Eric announced there was an opportunity to make money. Sir Reginald Bennett MP, a client of his, had informed him there was a plan afoot to import paintings of the masters, Renoir, Picasso etc that were in a gallery in France and were to be imported over the weekend and sold to waiting collectors at an already agreed price. We were told the scheme was run by Principality Finance who had millionaire investors. The offer from Sir Reginald was to invest £10,000 that would be repaid with a substantial profit within a week. Seemed too good to be true so we invested. Another message from Sir Reg, it was possible to increase our stake to £20,000 and that we did. (It is difficult to imagine five, so called intelligent men, doing such a thing). Monday came and there was a message that the main person putting the deal together had been found dead and no paintings had been found. I didn't believe it and wanted to see the body but it was true. The famous liquidation firm, Cork Gully, were called in to investigate. Their final report was that they had followed up every avenue but no paintings were found and the huge sums invested had disappeared.

An expensive lesson, so remember, 'if it sounds too good to be true, it isn't'.

Bernard Pendry

Xxxxxxxxxxx

Over the years Eric retired, Kanti move to Putney to be with Richard Atkins, Gordon Silver became a partner, married Anne Marie the practice manager, had a baby and moved on, Dick Levett divorced re married retired to north Cyprus, died leaving a financial mess. I split with Richard so in the end there was just Chris Mason, Mike Gibbons and me then I retired selling the practice to those two.

Commuting to central London was a chore. Right outside our offices at 3/4 Great Marlborough Street there was a motorbike bay so I thought 'why not'. I contacted my old boyhood friend, Babe Dodsworth who had always been into motorbikes and asked his advice thinking that a 125cc would be OK. His advice was that for the type of motoring I was intending I needed something more solid and with his help in 1977 I bought a Honda 400*4 with full fairing. Then for nearly 3 years I travelled to and from town on the bike in all kinds of weather and enjoyed the freedom one felt being able to get through no matter what. That was until one February evening coming home from work down the main A3 (at that time not a dual carriage way) approaching the Robin Hood round-a-bout a car swerved right in front of me so I pulled out and accelerated to find myself flying through the air then bouncing along the road with the bike scraping along beside me. After about 50 yards I came to a halt, got up, ran around like a chicken with its head chopped off but didn't feel anything broken or painful but some concerned passer-by had called an ambulance so off to Kingston Hospital I went for a check-up. All OK. Back home the kids and some friends joined me in the car and off we went to inspect the bike and try to find out what had happened. It turned out that during the daytime a lorry had demolished the keep left bollards leaving just the prominent curb in the middle of the road and the temporary lighting had failed. I thought about suing the council but they agreed to pay for the damage and a small compensation.

Then one icy winters morning I set off sliding and slipping, when approaching the Tolworth round-a-bout I thought "what the hell are you doing?" turned round back home and that was my last trip to town on the bike.

It was after the bike incident that I really made plans to relocate my section to near home and purchased the freehold of 124 Ewell Road, Surbiton leaving the other partners to run the London office. It was in October 1980 that we moved in and this certainly changed my life notably when young Sue Bunning, one of the helpers and I started an affair.

Everything went according to plan, I had two excellent managers Fran *a would be hippy* who was a tax expert and Alan Stevenson who went on to run his own business. In about 1990 Mike and Chris enquired about getting a share of the business so we met. My initial reaction was "why'" but at the meeting it hit me "why not let them have the whole of the London business it's time I considered retiring?" Their response was that they couldn't afford to. I said we could come to a deal which we did, part of which was they took over the responsibility of paying Eric Nabarros pension. They went on to run and expand the business over many years.

A few years later I sold 124 and bought 300/2 Ewell Road and 3/4 Sage Yard. Some of the space was used as my office, the rest let out.

I sold the Surbiton practice for peanuts and retired age 54.

It would be remiss of be not to record a late tribute to Ralph Leach my office manager. It was years later after I had retired and Ralph had died that I realised how he had taken so many burdens off my shoulders, he dealt with all the staff, organised the work schedule, ran the mortgage business and never complained. I did offer him a bonus depending on results but his response was that he was quite happy with his salary.

Bernard Pendry

CHAPTER 17

THE JOYS OF SQUASH

WIMBLEDON SQUASH & BADMINTON CLUB

1954 to 1971

Friend Ginge (Arthur Richardson) and I (age 18) read an advert in a local newspaper inviting people to try playing squash at Wimbledon Squash & Badminton Club. Neither of us had any idea about squash but we went along and thoroughly enjoyed it. They had a joining fee offer so we decided one of us would join and the other come along as a guest until we were certain it was the game for us. We spun a coin; I won so I was the member. This arrangement didn't last long because not long after Ginge had a serious injury when he was knocked off his scooter and ended in hospital for months. On recovery his legs were so bad he never played squash again.

I soon got in with a crowd consisting of Roger Board, Dave Timperley, John Harris, John Upton and others who regularly played every Monday and Thursday evenings, most prized time being 6.45. We all had our own ways to secure this time, mine being for both my secretary and myself on separate phones to continually phone until one of us got through.

With this little crowd we would go off to some upmarket restaurant either locally or many times up to Chelsea. I will always remember the very first time I accompanied this crowd, it was in a chintzy restaurant in Wimbledon Village quite smarter than anything I had experienced and a quick look at the menu told me I could be out of my league as the prices on the menu were higher than I had ever seen but it did not seem to faze any of the others who ordered fillet steak, Dover sole and the likes followed by wines and liqueurs. I quickly came to the conclusion that if I wanted to be part of the group I had to let them know that I would pay for what I ordered, which was pork fillet (delicious) and a couple of glasses of wine. No one raised an eyebrow and this was my policy for many years to come and we had many good times.

I could recount many stories but a particularly humorous one was in one of the swanky Chelsea restaurants, Dave Timperley, noted for getting inebriated on a couple of glasses of lager, managed to bring himself together when Fanny Craddock (the leading TV cook at the time) came floating in and wandered up to the manager for a chat. On the way out Dave stopped her and said "Fanny I so enjoy your programs and your advice on how to cook chips was amazing". I still don't know if this was a wind-up but she loved the comment and they chatted for some time.

On another occasion we agreed to go to a restaurant in Putney and from the start Roger and Dave decided it was a race and off they set in their sporty cars. Up Wimbledon Hill and flying across Wimbledon Common with Dave thinking it was Roger on his tail when the police flashed a sign for him to pull over. He was escorted to the police station where he was asked to take a blood test. He refused until a doctor was present. When one arrived about 20 minutes later Dave had been in the toilets drinking galleons of water, which presumably saved him being found over the limit.

This enjoyable time came to an end when right opposite my house they built the Mid Surrey Squash Club on a corner of The Old Haileybarians Cricket pitch

MID SURREY SQUASH CLUB

The club opened in 1970. I continued on at Wimbledon for a year but the attraction of just being able to wander across the road was too great. This opened a whole new chapter the likes of which I had never experienced before. It was not just a squash club but a major watering hole for fun and games, card schools every Friday night followed by a wander over to 'Argys' the local Indian restaurant then back to my house for more serious cards normally 3 card brag. My kids loved these nights benefiting from the money they made from taking orders for Welsh rarebits, cheese

Bernard Pendry

on toast and other delights plus in the morning searching for dropped change.

The first manager was John Dalchoe who more often than not was pissed, the good thing being he was in favour of late afters. One early evening after a bout of drinking elsewhere he pulled himself up the stairs and in front of him were two young ladies sipping their lemonades, possible new members, he staggered over to them, plonked his hands on their table and in a slurred voice said "who the fuck are you". I don't think they visited the club again.

Many nights after a drink I would wander over home leaving Sheila and Pam to finish their bottle (or two) of wine. This night I got a slurred phone call from Dalchoe "you, your wife and her friend are barred" and he slammed down the phone. The ladies came home totally unconcerned. He didn't last long after that.

A memorable squash game was a league match against Pauline Evens, the best lady player in the club. I won the first 2 games and was coasting in the third with a crowd of ladies watching. Thinking I shouldn't be too hard, I took my foot off the pedal and never got another look in. So in the fifth game decider I was pleased when our time ran out with the score at 6/4 to her. This is a good lesson in life, when your winning put the boot in!

I held my 40th and 50th parties there, first a pyjama party then a Roman Toga party. At the 40th the invited had clubbed together and sent Alan Pratt to buy a present that he thought would be appropriate. So with everyone gathered I was presented with two parcels. Opening the first it was one of the early computer games, like table tennis with a ball going from side to side. The next present left me speechless (if you can believe that); on opening it I was faced looking at a false fanny plus vibrator. When it was announced that Alan had purchased it with a cheque signed 'A Pratt' it caused many laughs but what use was it to a healthy 'young' man? The last I saw of it, it was tide to the bumper of Ray's car on the way home from a Mid Surrey v Fraser Court weekend away.

At the 50th Mum and aunt Floss were present and they were rather shocked when a stripper came on and did all sorts of things strippers do!

Another highlight was Joe Cocker's use of the Club throughout the 80s when he stayed with me.

Most of the members were locals but one Roland Hindle was Australian and when we planned to have a BBQ he said "leave it to me as I know how steaks should be cooked" So OK. Earlier in the day, round the side of the club, he had dug a pit into which he inserted coals, put the steaks over and covered it with earth. The evening was in merry spirit with much dancing and high jinx when someone enquired when would the steaks be ready? Roland was nowhere in the club but was found staring at uncooked steaks in his opened pit. Mournfully he admitted he had used the wrong coals that had gone out. I can't remember exactly what happened, maybe we sent out for fish & chips however we never saw Roland again. Such a shame as he was a friendly guy and a pretty good squash player.

Squash was a game that took off in the 70s, Mid Surrey opened with 4 courts and over the next few years expanded to 10. Slowly it closed courts to make way for a snooker table, dance studios and 3 went to build a swimming pool. It then changed hands to become a fitness club, no smoking, no after hours and now no courts. Sad.

Sometime later I started playing doubles at The Royal Automobile Club and continued for a few years until Old Father Time told me it was time to stop.

It is a game I recommend to everyone.

OLD SQUASH MATES

CHAPTER 18

RAY SAUNDERS – A MAN OF MANY PARTS

I first met Ray when he started dating Eileen Pemble, the sister of my fiancé Sheila and we soon discovered we were both boys from Fulham. His life story so far was that he was brought up in a block of council flats in a not too lugubrious part of Fulham with Mum, Dad and two sisters, was the only boy in the block to attend grammar school so took a lot of stick as the only one who had to wear a uniform. I think this formed his strong character. Having left school his first job was pasting up advertising posters soon followed by joining the Metropolitan Police where he had no wish for promotion content to play football for division and nationally. He said he was always the penalty taker and never missed one. He tells stories of how he wandered the street of Soho at night and all the antics he and his mates got up to.

In those early days the four of us spent a great deal of time in each others company, going on holidays, playing cards, trips in my 1928 Austin 7 and going to dances. It was on the way home from a dance at Chelsea Town Hall that the half shaft in the Austin went and we had to push it home to Ringmer Avenue. Oh! Happy days.

I regularly played golf at the municipal courses in Richmond Park and I talked Ray into giving it a try. This was the start of his incredible long journey in the golfing world as how a young lad from a council flat in Fulham could rise to become the leading figure in amateur world golf, Captain of The English Golf Union. I suggested to Ray that he write a book of this incredible journey but he wasn't interested. Maybe one day I'll attempt writing it.

From Richmond Park he joined Mid Kent Golf Club, and although he

Bernard Pendry

never joined the committee he became involved in organizing teams and inter club tournaments. I do not know the facts but he came to the notice first of The Kent Golf Union then The English Golf Union where he became a committee member eventually becoming the Captain. This earned him the right for he and Eileen to attend The Masters in Atlanta, Georgia. He also studied to become one of the leading referees in amateur golf. He recounts that he was the only non-public school person in the whole system.

When Eileen and Ray married they rented a flat in Streatham and soon moved to Kent so we didn't see much of them except at Christmas when they stayed with us at our wonderful house, 30 Ruxley Lane with their children Claire and Howard making a complete family occasion. Occasionally we all went on away trips first to a holiday camp in Prestatyn, north Wales. We hired a people carrier large enough for both families to get in and tied a board; actually it was an old double bed headboard with in large letters MERRY CHRISTMAS EVERY ONE attracting many waves along the way. All five kids enjoyed dressing up for fancy dress parade.

Next it was to a hotel in Bournemouth where I can still see father-in-law Ted dressed as father Christmas sitting on an upstairs loo waiting for his grandchildren to arrive and latterly The Bell Hotel in Brighton where a highlight was watching a mass of people swimming in the sea amongst Father Christmases on paddle boards.

When Ray was in the police he got friendly with Dev Pritchard, a young lad up from Wales, who had joined the police just to get a feel of life in the capital. His family were farmers who transported milk to the city so I think were quite well off. Anyway it was clear that Dev had no intention of staying in the police too long and was on the lookout for a business to get into. He located a large shop for sale in Eynsford, Kent, and decided to buy it and open a confectionary shop. Much work was needed and he tempted Ray to leave the police and concentrate on getting the shop ready for opening. I am not sure what happened next but the two of them ran the business for many years and later opened a warehouse in Leytonstone specifically for the tobacco trade, which grew substantially.

In a conversation with Ray I asked if he had any shares in the company.

None. So I explained that if the business were sold he would be entitled to nothing. He asked if I would have a word with Dev, which I did over a nice lunch. I discussed the purpose of the meeting i.e. getting Ray an interest in the company. It went like this me "the way I see it is that the business is made up of 3 parts, your money, your and Ray's input, so in fairness it should be a third each". Well he nearly fell off his chair exclaiming, "no way, why should Ray be entitled to any shares?" In the end all he would do was give Ray 5% without any payment, which I reported to Ray. And this is how it continued up to the time Dev decided to sell the business for I do not know what.

I had had no dealings with the business and the first thing I knew was when Ray contacted me to say Dev was threatening him with a court case. What seemed to have happened was Ray, being a signatory on the company's bank account, had taken a third of the sale price and Dev wanted it back. By this time Ray had started a business supplying cigarettes to machines in pubs and the like. This didn't work out so he invested in a franchise for Bath Doctor a business where baths could be resprayed but there were always problems and he had lost his money. He made all kind of threats of what he would like to do to Dev but I explained that he had no defense to Dev's claim and that if it went to court, he would lose. So reluctantly he asked if I would talk to Dev. This I did and we had a convivial meeting that swayed one way and another him trying to hold his ground some £15,000 me trying to beat him down and explaining that Ray had lost whatever money he had taken. I got him down to £3,200 provided it was paid within the week. I chatted to Ray who thought he was being screwed and in any event could not raise the money. So I agreed to loan him the £3,200 that settled the case, which was paid back when Ray sold the apartment he owned in Spain.

Dev went on to better things building up a chain of nursing homes that he sold for £32,000,000 and moved to Gibraltar. I occasionally visited him with Pam and he always took us to the local casino giving her a 100 euro chip to gamble. Even if she won he would not take a euro back. On one of these trips he did mention what it was like working with Ray, he said he was dogmatic but was a positive promoter of the business.

Ray became an agent for The Sun Life of Canada but it so happened my partners and I were looking for someone to run our company Regent Financial Management Limited, which specialized in the pension/ mortgage business so I suggested he might like to join us. He did and made a great success soon being promoted to managing director with a gift of 25% of the shares. All went well for many years until the new rules made Ray spend most of his time on administration so he decided to retire.

With the millennium approaching many people thought what could we do to celebrate. Well the four of us booked a trip on The Canadian Pacific Railway travelling from Toronto across to Vancouver, an experience of a lifetime. I had never experienced cold like it was in Toronto; it was a pleasure to go down in the underground shopping centers for some warmth. It was fun watching Eileen and Pam trying on very expensive beautiful fur coats in an upmarket store in Vancouver.

We both were reasonable squash players our clubs being Fraser Court for Ray and Mid Surrey Squash club for me. Ray thought it would be a good idea if we arranged some inter club matches possibly including some golf. As a starter I took a team over to Kent, Nick Preece a member of my team was staying at Mick Jennings house just over the road from Ray's and a funny thing happened. Waking he headed for the toilet but had to rush back as the alarm clock was going but no amount of hitting would stop it. There was a kerfuffle going on outside and looking out there were a few neighbors gesticulating. He then discovered it wasn't the alarm clock the culprit being the burglar alarm. Mick had left early for work before the day's festivities and forgot to tell Nick about the alarm.

For about ten years Ray organized long weekend tournaments for both clubs and every one was a merry riot with friendly but competitive rivalry. Again this could be a book on its own with so many happy stories. Not only did we compete in squash and golf but there was football, cricket, rowing, bat & trap (a Kentish game), snooker, darts and no doubt some other activities that now escape me.

On one of these occasions Brian Broadhurst, a member of my team, came up from playing snooker with Ray in a most aggressive and angry manner, accusing Ray of cheating and was all ready to go home. It took Roy Oldaker ages walking him up and down the car park to settle him.

Ray enquired what was happening and when I explained the situation he said he knew Brian was upset when after a foul shot he had asked Brian to replay the shot, which is well within the rules. Apparently Brian hadn't a clue and thought Ray was cheating.

A little incident that highlights Ray's competitiveness was when we entered a doubles squash competition at Croydon Squash Club. The first and second rounds were on a Sunday and winners had to compete on the Monday. We won our first match then had to play the second round where we were evenly matched. The score was 2 sets all when I reminded Ray that neither of us wanted to return on the Monday so we ought to lose. He nodded but when the score got to 7 all he could not hold back so I just stood against the back wall watching him burst a blood vessel. Fortunately we did lose.

They had lived for many years in Dicken's Close, Hartley a nice detached house. The story goes that they (or Ray) decided to move to a bungalow as Eileen had trouble climbing the stairs but without showing her the new bungalow he purchased it. Lovely bungalow ample space the only drawback was that you had to climb a considerable flight of stairs to get to the front door. So Eileen would leave her shopping at the bottom for Ray to collect later. Sometime later he was fed up with having to clear leaves in the autumn so they moved again but this time to an apartment and there was a lift to the front door. What I found funny was considering his reason for moving i.e. the leaves; there he was thigh deep in the river clearing weeds.

Ray's daughter Claire was over from Hong Kong with her family, Pam and I were invited to join them for lunch at a smart restaurant in Westerham, Kent. It was great seeing them all again but unfortunately Pam was in an advance stage with cancer, which put a bit of a damper on the occasion.

Apart from being a tremendous organiser Ray is a great raconteur and storyteller, get him to tell you the story of the Winky, Wonky Donkey.

MILLENNIUM RAIL JOURNEY ACROSS CANADA

DAD & RAY AS FLANAGAN & ALLAN

CHAPTER 19

MIKE HOLLOWAY – THE ENIGMA

THE START

Sometime in the early seventies I got talking to this new neighbour, Pam, who had moved into 21 Ruxley Lane, right opposite my house. She had on this incredibly short hot pants, not that that had anything to do with it, and we started chatting. First question where is your husband. He was away working for Hilton Hotel's European branch based in Nairobi and only came home occasionally to mow the lawn and socialize with old friends. I think this is why he got the nickname 'The Seldom Seen Kid'.

On one of these rare visits we met, he was a very convivial chap full of Bon Homie and we got on well, started playing a bit of golf, had a few drinks in the local squash club and discussed life. Pam and Sheila became firm friends and spent much time in each other's company.

BUT THERE ARE SO MANY STORIES.

READ ON

THE PUB GAME

1976. Mike returned to the UK with Iona, a beautiful ex airhostess with an endearing Edinburgh brogue with whom they had daughter Tara, to run The Market Hotel in Alton, Hampshire. This was a cosy traditional pub, even had a ninepin bowling alley out the back. I became their accountant and when things seemed to be going OK, against my better judgment, he took the tenancy of The White Horse Pub in Holybourne about seven miles away. In November 1979 I had lunch with Iona and it was clear that things were not going well and in 1980 he got out of the pub game leaving Iona running the Market Hotel. Don't know what happed to The White Horse, must have run away!

MY FIRST HELPING HAND

1986. Mike now out of pubs was trying to get something going in the travel industry and needed an office. So I invited him to use space in my offices provided he helped me promote The Golf Club Great Britain plus I would pay him £1,000 per month. Things went well and he got a contract with the Portuguese Tourist Board to promote Pearls of Portugal Tour. He told them about his tie up with the GCGB and persuaded them to put up a weeks holiday for two as a prize. He organised some sort of raffle and guess who won it? Surprise, surprise, my wife Sheila who took daughter Nicola on a magical holiday touring the north of Portugal.

HIS TRAVEL BUSINESS

A year or so later Mike had changed jobs, now employed by a travel company based in Greece who owned The Cavorie Hotel in Athens. Somehow he arranged for Pam, her kids David and Tracy plus Sheila, kids Mark, Michael, Nicola and me to spend a fortnight there for free. Not knowing Mike very well I took this with a pinch of salt and took lots of cash if things didn't turn out. Mike met us at the airport, I hired a car and off we went. What a surprise not only were we welcomed to the hotel but shown into the two master suites on the top floor, incredible. What a super holiday but didn't see much of Mike as he was always off somewhere else. We had a trip to the Parthenon and an amusing thing happened. As we were approaching this majestic building we heard Mike Pendry say to Tracy "Incredible, look at this" thinking he was referring to the Parthenon but when Tracy enquired he said "have you seen the size of these ants?"

May 1987. When Nick Preece sold Redmans Estate Agents for many millions he wanted to repay me for what he saw as my acting for him in the many negotiations as beyond my professional duty and consulted Mike for his ideas. Mike arranged a long weekend at the Monte Carlo Beach Hotel for the four of us. What a place, so expensive thankfully they had guests menus so we didn't have to look at the prices, there was no way we were going to get inebriated. The hotel did have a strip of beach that had private huts, Nick enquired about hiring one but declined when told the cost for a day was £500. For a laugh Pam added a portion of prunes to their breakfast menu hanging out side their bedroom door. Nick was not impressed, it cost £22.

Oct. 1987. For his 50th birthday Mike arranged for a party of about 40 of us to spend a few days at The El Paraiso Hotel in Bena Vista, southern Spain. What a tremendous fun affair it was, some golf, lots of swimming and dancing and a "bit" of drinking. We all paid Mike our dues only later to learn that he knocked the hotel.

NEXT HELPING HAND

1995 November. Mike out of his luck again I let him use my office to run his business Sports Marketing & Promotions with Roz again to help run The GCGB. Kate and Kathy, who ran the show, were not impressed. Roz's dad John was also in the office, he had recently invented a board game based on cricket. Mike took this to a promotion company who bought the rights for £15,000. John never saw a penny of this.

Dec. 1995. I accompanied Mike to a meeting with The British Legion at their offices in Pall Mall where he interested them in sponsoring a National Golf Tournament, which they fell for and later gave him a budget of £20,000. With Roz he set up an office in Norfolk, ran a few golf days in 1996. Things couldn't have gone well because he disappeared. Son Dave had collected him and he spent some months living with Dave and wife, Jenny, before transferring to Daughter Tracy's.

THE THEFT

February 1999, wintering at Macarena C in Spain, I get a phone call from Kate, the lady who was running The GCGB for me, that the new computer and printer we had bought a couple of months earlier had disappeared. The police had been called but because there was no break in no insurance claim was valid. It was a total mystery so the only thing to do was buy new ones. Unfortunately we had only just employed someone to reload all the information into the new system so he was reemployed. Many months went past when Roz phoned me to say Mike had offered her a new computer but when she started it, up came The GCGB so she refused it. I asked why it had taken so long to inform me. Her answer was that the police had been after Mike, who by then had disappeared back to Surrey hiding from a case bought by The British Legion for their £20,000. I fathomed that Mike must have been staying with Tracy, who was our office cleaner, and used her key to get in.

Many more months later, and another stay at Macarena, I get another phone call from Kate to say that the home post taken in by Carol a friend, contained an envelope in which was £1,500 and the writing on the cover just said Bernard in writing that she said was Mike's. I told her to put it in a draw to await my return. On my return I showed the envelope to Pam who confirmed the writing was Mike's. It was totally unbelievable to conclude that Mike had any conscience, but maybe I was wrong. Thinking of the upheaval this had caused to Kate and her helper Kathleen I gave them £500 to share.

A couple of years earlier I had done a deal with Graham White, friend, butcher and client who was negotiating a property deal that I would do the tax planning for a fee if the deal went ahead.

Sitting in my office it dawned on me that Graham still owed me and reached for the phone to chase him up. Just as it started ringing the thunder struck, that £1,500 was nothing to do with Mike, it was Graham's

HIS WOMEN

Pam was the first and tells the story of their early married life with their two children nicely settled in their cosy house in Shropshire and Mike in business with his best friend, Dave Baddock when there was a knock on the door. It was the bailiffs, the business had gone belly up and they wanted money. Horrendous situation, Dave emigrated to Australia leaving Mike to face the music. I don't know what happened but this is when they moved to 21 Ruxley Lane.

They divorced September 1975 but instead of agreeing to pay maintenance he arranged for the brewery to grant her a license of The Hop Bag Pub in Farnham, Surrey. The fact that she had no idea how to run a pub was of no consequence.

Then **Iona.** See The Pub Game above.

Next came **Sue**? a beautiful blonde, and they bought a large house just outside Kingston, Surrey where they lived for a few years doing lots of entertaining. Sue was a qualified clerk to the court but things went horribly wrong when she got into financial problems because he had signed many cheques forging her signature, which resulted in her going bankrupt and ended their marriage.

Jackie Goodram joined Mike in his travel business IBIT along with son Dave. They were an item but cannot remember much about her.

Roz and Mike lived as a couple in Kingston where they held many parties in 1995 and 1996. They soon moved to Norfolk where she continued to assist him in his travel business connected with The British Legion golf days.

Roz returned to Surrey again to help Mike who was now using my office together with her father who had developed a cricket board game, which Mike took to a publisher of games and got an advance of £15,000. The game sold reasonably well but Roz's father never saw a penny. See her involvement in The Theft above.

Angie. A few of us were dining in the local Greek restaurant; we left leaving Mike chatting to this charming lady. Next thing we knew he had moved in with her. A year or two later she sold up her fashion shop and house and they moved to Condom a few miles south of Toulouse where they still live to this day.

THE WEYBRIDGE VENTURE

With friend Trevor, Mike had taken a license of a restaurant in Weybridge, Surrey about the same time as Iona was selling up The Market Hotel, so he did a deal with her that he would take all her furniture and fitting to install in the new place at a price that never got paid. Anyway Pam & I were playing crazy golf in Spain and got chatting to a couple in the bar. Talking about golf we found we had been a members of the same golf society and I mentioned that Mike had also been a member. Well, before I finished both Trevor and his wife went rigid. They explained that they had been the friends and had gone into business with Mike in a restaurant venture. Trevor had got fed up with the way Mike ran the place and had left. A year later he received a summons from the bank demanding £30,000. Apparently he was the guarantor for the bank overdraft that Mike had ranked up. Apparently they nearly went bankrupt.

MACARENA C.

Just after we bought it in July 1996, Mike drove down loaded with bits and pieces and joined Pam to put the house in order. We let him use it many times without charge even for electricity.

1999 THE REALISATION AS TO HIS EVIL CHARACTER

Throughout the year not only had we acted as friends, enjoying drinks with Pete and others, letting him stay the night as he had to get up early for a meeting and gave him funds to help with Renoirs. Also he was invited to my fabulous Stag Do and the following Wedding plus joining Pam and me for a holiday at Macarena C at the end of which he & I drove home taking 3 days in convivial company. In July when I got the payout from the Royal Automobile Club from selling off the motor recovery business, I gave him £500.

BOMB SHELL. The phone call from Roz as fully documented above in THEFT section. I felt physically sick.

To cap it all Mike had come into the office on 24th March asking if I would loan him £1,000 as he had urgent debts to pay and he would pay me back when his pension moneys came in a weeks time. Every bone in me said 'DON'T' but I relented and he gave me a Sports Promotions &

Associates cheque for £1,000 that is still bouncing around my office.

How can anyone, who has stolen valuable property, act so naturally as a friend? You fathom it out!

Xxxxxxxxxxxxxx

Many years have passed; I have relented and once more enjoy his company although any chance of a loan is out of the question!

All in all Mike was enjoyable to socialise with provided it did not include money or honesty.

CHAPTER 20

TRAGEDIES - 547,600,000 to 1.

TAYLOR

4th May 1995 My grandson Taylor was born to Nikki & Michael, a healthy baby who grew to be the most lovely grandchild who was interested in everything especially in his Dad's work in the landscaping business. He knew all the tractors, diggers etc and enjoyed going to work with his Dad. Pam & I looked after him on many occasions and always put on Bob the Builder shows. His brother Charlie came along on 19th July 1997 and they became great mates always playing together. Next was baby Olivia on 11th November1998.

On Friday 25th March 2000 Nikki asked if I could look after Taylor in the daytime. Because he had not gone to school as he felt poorly. Of course, and I had many hours with him, helping him with his homework, playing football in the garden he seemingly perfectly OK. The next Monday Taylor seemed OK but Nikki was preparing to take him to the doctors, she sat him in the lounge watching Bob-the Builder and went to make him a sandwich. When she returned Taylor was lying sideways just staring at the ceiling trance like and did not respond to anything. Horrified she immediately called an ambulance.

To go on is just painful. He was rushed to Epsom Hospital and all the family were alerted, both grandmothers looked after the siblings, granddad Terry flew back from his golfing holiday in Portugal, Pam and I visited him in hospital and were confused with all the machines he was wired up to. The experts at St. Georges Hospital tried everything and their early diagnosis was that it was not a virus but a form of epilepsy that can be treated. This gave such false hope and soon he was in a coma and started seizing. Members of the family spent days and nights at the hospital hoping for signs of improvement, there were none. He was transferred to The Children's Trust at Tadworth and again there were hopes he would recover some of his faculties in fact he did start saying Bob-the Builder, passed balls back and forth so fingers crossed. Again these hopes were false and things went from bad to worse, months and years passed. Michael studied the case files, had meetings with the medical experts trying to understand what had happened. No doubt his medical file is many feet thick but to what effect.

He is now 23, body wise OK but mentally little cognizance and living in a very well appointed nursing home in Shepperton visited regularly by Mum, Dad, Olivia and Charlie.

The pain caused to Nikki & Michael is unimaginable and poor Charlie lost his big brother playmate. Olivia was too young to understand the situation but as she grew older the tragedy has had its effect. The future is hard to foretell.

July 2001. A few family and friends arranged a charitable cycle ride from The Monkey Puzzle Pub adjacent to Chessington World of Adventure to Brighton. Jake and husband Gary, the seasoned cyclists, led the way avoiding the major roads and all went well until they reached Ditchling Beacon, a notoriously steep hill, twisting and turning to the top of the Surrey Hills. Only four of the riders made the top without stopping and poor Mark, who had borrowed an off road bike, had not practiced, had cycled to the start down from home in Banstead, was finding it difficult. I offered to get his bike into my car for the hill climb but he would have none of it and walked all the way up. They all got to Brighton safely, had a good evening celebrating, dossed in various B & Bs and in the morning loaded the bikes onto a friend's truck and caught the train home. Raised quite a few thousands for The Children's" Trust.

HARVEY

22nd October 2008 my grandson Harvey was born to daughter Nicola and Neil, their second child after Tess, nearly 3 years old. He was ostensibly a healthy baby, lots of chuckles and smiles.

On Wednesday 4th February 2009 they called round, I had taken Tess to the local swings, Pam was cuddling Harvey when for some reason he had a massive crying fit but soon settled down. March 7th Harvey was taken to Epsom Hospital as he was having fits and Nicola stayed the night. March 13th Nicola phones to say that Harvey is under control. March 17th Pam and I holidaying at Macarena get a phone call from Nicola saying Harvey is having many fits, got home as soon as I could. Rushed to hospital to meet Nicola and Neil. Baby Harvey gave such a lovely smile it was hard to believe that anything serious could be wrong but his seizures continue. He was transferred to St Georges Hospital in the same ward as Taylor was in 9 years ago. I am not aufait with the details but poor Harvey did not improve and to stop the seizures had an operation to take part of his brain away. I don't know what they expected but it has left him both mentally and physically damaged. Because his seizures have stopped there is no reason for him to go into care so he lives at home with much support from the authorities e.g. a lift has been installed for ease to get him to his bedroom, a wet room, harness winch to get him into his chair and buggies, a large wagon for transporting him and occasional carers.

This trauma could have split the family but they have pulled together and after much pondering decide to try for another child and along came Cali on 29th July 2011 so once again a happy family.

Many trials have been carried out to see if there is any connection between these two conditions but nothing has shown up.

The experts at The Children's Trust said the chance of Taylor's illness was 740,000 to 1. If the same statistic applies to Harvey you arrive at 547,600,000 to 1.

Who arrives at these statistics?

GLADYS

My sister Glad (baptized Gladys Vera Marie) was born on 13th May 1928 (when my Mum and Dad were still living at Eardley Crescent) so by the time I came along her problems were well known. She was trapped mentally and physically in the mental age of a 5 years old. I remember her as such a loving person who enjoyed helping Mum. She was always singing children's songs such as 'H.A.P.P.Y.'. I don't know when, why or how she disappeared from home, on reflection it may have been because of Mum being called up for war work.

She spent the rest of her life in various homes, Shepton Mallet, Caterham ending at The Manor, Epsom just up the road from where I now live. I sometimes accompanied our parents on visits and Glad who always greeted us with a big smile and hugs all round. Going to these types of hospital is always a little uneasy, as there are many characters that you do not meet elsewhere. She died at age 40 from Pancreatic cancer.

Bernard Pendry

GROUP CHARITY RIDE TO BRIGHTON

HALFWAY THERE

CHAPTER 21

CANCER: THE DREADED BIG "C"

The three years tortuous journey to a tragic end

All my life, like many people, I knew there was such a thing called cancer but had never come in contact with anything to do with it. Unfortunately, this ostrich like attitude was shattered.

My second wife Pam was a healthy 70 years old, we played tennis, walked went on many holidays and life was good.

20th July 2010. Getting home from a round of golf at The Addington Golf Club there were messages on my phone from both my son-in-laws, Dave and Pete to inform me that Pam had been rushed to St. Helier Hospital. Apparently she had gone to our doctor Holbrook with severe stomach pains who immediately told her to go to the hospital. Neighbour Joan had accompanied her and after an examination they suspected it could be an appendicitis although it would be rare in someone of her age, so she was kept in for further tests. With a bundle of items that Pam wanted, off I went. She was in good humour but very tender and told me they were to do keyhole surgery that night to define the problem. Yes it turned out to be her appendix but there were also tumours that they removed.

22nd July. The operation went well, still sore but relieved to know what it was.

25th July. Pam comes home. Temporary bedroom down stairs. Comfy.

30th July. Severe stomach pains, just resting.

3rd August. All stitches out. Feeling better. Hoping life gets back to normal.

23rd August. Trip to Sutton Hospital to see the specialist, Kim. Not good news there is still a part of the tumour left in her colon so further tests are necessary. (The first time we had heard the word "tumour" brought worrying thought of the big C). Pam was in shock and very tearful. Now all the family were on red alert.

25th August. Full body scan at St. Helier.

27th August. Meeting with Dr. Raja at The Clockhouse Medical Centre. He explained the MRI scan had shown further tests were needed which meant a camera procedure in the anus and a look at the colon. More stress and worries.

1st September. The Clockhouse for blood tests to see if her kidneys are strong enough to take the purging powders prior to the telescopy.

5th September. Pam had to take diarrhea tablets to clear her stomach ready for the Colonoscopy tomorrow. A night of running to the toilet, more pain, more anguish.

6th September. St. Anthony's Hospital for the Colonoscopy after which Dr. Raja gave us the good news that Pam was cancer free. What relief and she couldn't wait to give the good news to all the family. Celebrations followed.

20th September. Back again at St. Anthony's where Dr. Raja said that to be on the safe side Pam should have another scan just to make certain there were no cells that had gone undetected and to be sure he recommended an operation. He confirmed categorically there was nothing life threatening.

26th September. Pam's 74th birthday.

25th October. Another scan at St. Helier.

29th October. Meeting with Dr. Raja at Cottage Hospital who explained that nothing had shown up on the scans but recommended a "clean out" operation went ahead. (In hindsight should have called for a second opinion).

5th November. Took Pam to St. Anthony's Hospital in preparation for Dr. Raja's operation tomorrow, which he said, would be straightforward.

6th November. Dr. Raja said how well the operation had gone although it took over 4 hours to remove both ovaries and stem cells.

7th November. Pam now in intensive care, wired up and very emotional realizing how severe the operation was. Her stomach is in a horrendous mess; I have photos showing the totally ugly state.

15th November. Pam comes home after spending days in lots of pain with both her stomach and now her back. Dr. Raja said her stomach was doing fine but had no answer as to her back pains.

Weeks followed with Pam in agony and taking strong painkillers. Plus her asthma has got worse.

6th December. Another meeting with Dr. Raja who explained the operation went well and **she was clear of cancer** but said she should now visit Professor Cunningham the top cancer specialist at The Royal Marsden Hospital in Sutton. (All very confusing).

8th December. We visited Prof. Cunningham at Royal Marsden Hospital in Sutton. He said (categorically) that Pam does not have cancer but went on to explain about seedlings and recommended chemotherapy. This was the start of a horrendous chain of events that went on all through 2011, 2012 and 6 months of 2013 with chemo, radiotherapy masses of hospital visits, drugs, continual pains and listlessness, more operations.

2011

2nd February. Pam not feeling well so phoned Dr. Raja who recommended going to Marsden. This resulted in her being kept in for 2 days for observation.

7th February. Feeling much better.

12th July. Called to a meeting with Prof. Cunningham who confirmed Pam has 3 cancer cells in the lining of her stomach. This change in his attitude was most frightening. It is now the start of many sessions of chemotherapy

22nd July. Royal Marsden Hospital in the Fulham Road to see Mr. Khan to discuss an operation to insert a port for the chemo. He inserted one on 26th.

27th July. Series of chemotherapy starts.

3rd August. Marsden to see Dr. Tait chief radiologist to discuss treatment when chemotherapy ends. She confirmed that the 3 tumours being treated are not life threatening.

6th October. They stop chemotherapy because the pains in Pam's stomach continue to be severe. Now further examinations.

19th October. Marsden to see Dr. Suad to discuss PET scan results. Tumours only slightly down so recommend radiotherapy under Dr. Tait.

2nd November. Met Dr. Tait who said the side effects of radiotherapy would be minimal. Treatment starts. (Her stomach pains continue severe).

14th December. Marsden. Dr. Tait thinks Pam has improved but organises another PET Scan

2012

11th January. Marsden. Dr. Tait and results of PET SCAN. Tumours not gone but seem dormant and says no need to worry. (None of this relieved the pains in her stomach).

21st March 2012. Saw Dr. Tait to discuss PET Scan results. Tumours still there but no activity. Sound positive.

21st April. St. Anthony's Hospital where Dr. Raja operates. (Did not improve anything)

21st May. Marsden and Dr. Tait for results of blood test. Bad news she has cancer seedlings in her stomach. More chemo follows.

10th October 2012. Prof. Cunningham pleased with Pam's progress and confirmed that the scan showed nothing serious.

31st October 2012. Meeting with Prof. Cunningham and his team. Not good news, Pam is not responding to treatment and they had no suggestions so basically we are on our own with only HOPE left.

6th November. Marsden to see Dr. Alex who was concerned that Pam had not had injection for a clot for 3 days. An ultrasound check showed all clear.

13th November. BOMB SHELL. Dr. Alex phoned re results of scan, tumours have grown and attached to her liver hence it is terminal. We were in shock and in tears.

2013

During these dark days we investigated many alternative medicines, had a second opinion in Harley Street, comforted each other as best we could but through all the pain and suffering it was difficult.

So what now, must enjoy the time that is left to us? First we booked a business class flight to Orlando to take up Sally & Nick Preece's offer to spend a fortnight with them at their house in The Villages, Florida. We had a happy time with Pam enjoying driving their golf buggy into town.

Next a Caribbean cruise starting at Barbados. Pam was in good spirits and with the aid of a wheel chair we missed out on nothing.

Then we had two weeks at our beautiful house in Calahonda, Spain where we used to spend the 3 winter months. It was sad saying farewell to the many friends we had made.

9th May 2013. Pam spent a week in The Princes Alice Hospice in Esher, Surrey for a thorough check up and thoroughly enjoyed it. Dr. Amanda was a great comfort. (It was Dr. Amanda who inspired me to get an electric bike)

29th May 2013. What a change, Pam was up at 5.30 feeling good, ate well and was generally in good spirits. But this was a false dawn and she was taken into hospital.

17ᵗʰ June Our Dr. Holbrook visited Pam and tried to comfort her. He visited many times, a true saint.

28ᵗʰ June Pam was in so much pain she accepted the offer to go into Esher Princes Alice Hospice again for a week's convalescence. She felt so comfortable in the excellent room allocated to her that when her time came for a final visit she had no fears.

1ˢᵗ July Pam was ambulanced to the Hospice fearing she would not see our house again.

7ᵗʰ July. A very sunny Sunday. Early in the morning Pam was tired and weary but enjoyed a cuddle and a kiss. As the day wore on she improved and visitors started to arrive, granddaughter Lucie, Eileen & Ray, Nikki, Mike, Charlie, Olivia plus dogs Jemma & Louis, Nicola & Neil, daughter Tracy & Pete. It was so warm I asked Pam if she would like to go into the garden and with a wheel chair we set up in a secluded corner and it was truly amazing how Pam responded to every one considering how ill and out of it she had been for months.

14ᵗʰ July Sunday morning Dave & Tracy phoned to say how Pam was slipping away. I broke all speed records to get to the Hospice but was just too late. Pam had peacefully passed away. The Only comfort is that her three years of suffering had ended.

22ⁿᵈ July. The Funeral, extremely emotional for all although beautifully conducted by Deborah, a nature person, and super speeches by Mark who read my eulogy (I thought I could do it but was too emotional), David's letter to his Mum, Nicola on the joys of our two families, Charlie on behalf of the many grandchildren and a note from Mollie who is in the Far East. The wake was at Ewell Court House and after all the tears was a happy celebration of Pam's life.

My advice: steer clear of Dr. Raja and think twice before agreeing to either chemotherapy or radiotherapy.

CARIBBEAN, OUR LAST CRUISE

LAST CRUISE

CHAPTER 22

THE GREAT JOE COCKER

When I got the assignment to look after the affairs of Nigel Thomas, a manager of rock & Roll artists I had no idea why I had been picked because I had no idea whatsoever what the Music industry was about, I had never been to a gig, a concert, a music festival, rarely watched Top of the Pops and had no idea who Joe Cocker was. The only thing I was aware of was the huge success of The Beatles and The Rolling Stones. The last record I bought was Hank Williams, my favourite.

So how did it continue? Nigel Thomas had a few relatively unknown artists so affairs were very low key but somehow he learnt that Joe Cocker needed a manager so he sent a roadie named Plum to find him, which he did and Joe was signed up.

Now things really started happening and Nigel organised a 30 odd dates tour of the United States called "The Joe Cocker Tour". He assembled a group of players and off they went to Connecticut to rehearse. At this stage I was not involved.

After the first gig in Carnegie Hall, New York I got a phone call from Nigel, "Just how soon can you get out here, dealing with the twelve band members and the whole entourage is too much and I need you as the moneyman?" Having agreed my fee, the opportunity to visit the States was alluring so I was on the plane next day heading for Jacksonville, Florida and the Hilton Hotel. This was a hotel the likes of which I had never experienced, so palatial and rooms the size of our house.

Down for breakfast about 9.30 there were no people who looked like rock & rollers but soon a plump, short waitress with a jolly smile plopped down the obligatory coffee pot and asked what I would like for breakfast.

My words were "I'm starving so would like a big breakfast as you choose" and off she waddled to return a couple of minutes later with a plate piled with pancakes plus a jar of Maple Syrup. Not my expected egg, bacon, hash browns, mushrooms and baked beans. However they all went down as a pleasant new experience, one not to be repeated.

Soon a few people appeared and Nigel introduced me to Joe. He was just an ordinary guy and we sat chatting for over an hour and I got the distinct impression he was just one extremely nice fellow who would be easy to get along with. As I have said, I had no idea he was famous, had I known of his fame I may have been in awe.

My responsibilities was everything to do with finances, study every contract for the gigs and collect the money, pay weekly 'wages' to all the crew which consisted of 12 players, four roadies and another dozen of so who did something, and pay all expenses. Thank goodness I am a fast learner.

The players supporting Joe were Chris Stainton, his close friend, other members of The Grease Band, Neil Hubbard, Alan Spenner, Bruce Rowland, two who played with the Stones, Jim Price and Bobby Keys who I fell out with when he wanted more money no doubt to buy drugs, Felix Falcon a bongo player, a lovely little guy but so into drugs he died not long after and there were three lovely black lady singers including Viola Wills the only black lady I ever kissed.

So off we all set for my first 'gig'. I had no idea what to expect so was awe struck with the huge size of the arena, Joe's dressing room that could easily accommodate a dozen plus the crate of Dom Perignon champagne. The auditorium was packed and there was an audible expectant buzz and when Joe walked on the place erupted with cheers and hullaballoo.

Then the band struck up and the place rocked to music so loud the place shuddered. Not ever having heard Joe sing I was in awe, he was terrific and got huge applause for every song. Even mystified by Joe's antics on stage resembling having an epileptic fit (later mimicked by many imitators). After, a few of us assembled in his dressing room drinking the champagne and everything else that was supplied.

Every other gig was just as fantastic. The audiences loved him.

Bernard Pendry

Normally the crew except for the roadies travelled to the next gig in luxury coaches while the roadies packed up the gear into two trucks and drove. The exception was when Nigel hired a private plane and we flew into New Orleans. It was there that it came over to me just how famous Joe was as we alighted the plane to be met buy a New Orleans Jazz Band.

Other particularly memorable events.

The Hollywood Bowl a huge open-air arena and one night when the roadies were setting up the stage I wandered to the middle and staring out at the hordes taking their seats it came over to me how daunting it would be to perform in front of so many.

The Surfrider Hotel. The final gig was Hawaii and our hotel was right on Waikiki Beach. This put every other hotel we had stayed in to shame. From by balcony I could watch many surfers gliding in on the waves. So I thought why not me as I had done a little surfing in Weston-Super-Mare many years ago. So collecting one of the hotels surfboards I set out to join the surfers. Well I watched how they started before they stood up and whizzed towards shore. I tried and tried but not a single wave bothered to collect me and after struggling for ages had the ignominy of having to paddle back.

Joe swimming. Joe was so well known he wanted to get away so I took him and Eileen for a tour of the island looking for another beach. I didn't realise that like so many islands the beaches were few and far apart. After a while we did stop at an isolated very small beach and the waves were crashing in. Joe wanted to swim, he had no swimming trunks so he ripped off the bottoms of the trouser legs and was prepared to go. I was explaining to them both that the way to get past the waves was to dive straight into one, swim hard and come out the other side where it would be less rough. Eileen was first up, she rushed at a wave, got thrown into the air landing back on the beach. After a couple more tries she gave up. So I said to Joe "follow me and dive straight in when I do". All went to plan and we started to swim out. Soon he said to me "are you a good swimmer?" and to my "No" he said "let's start back". We were approaching the beach when a big wave picked him up and unceremoniously dumped him sprawling onto the beach. It was then clear he had no pants on and the ripped jeans did him no favours.

Love Beach, Nassau. At the end of the tour as a thanks, Joe invited a few of us to stay at six lodges on Love Beach, quite idyllic. Joe suggested I ask my wife, Sheila to join us, so a quick phone call, arrangements made and she was on the next plane out. There is the story of her attending a local gospel church and being asked to say hello to the congregation. I have vivid memories of her walking naked along the secluded beach.

Now a firm friendship was made and in the years that followed either he stayed with the family and me or we all visited him in various locations. The most fabulous was Hill House, in the mountains behind Santa Barbara, rented from Jane Fonda who we did see by the swimming pool. On one of these visits we got Joe to try his hand at golf. So son Mark drove our buggy while daughter Nicola drove Joe. He turned up wearing a bright baseball cap with silver wings. After teaching him what end of the club to hold we set off. Down the first hole his tee shot went straight left ending up against a fence. I said just drop out but he continued to swipe at the ball eventually putting out for a 13. Did it get any better? No but we had lots of laughter.

When staying with us his favourite watering hole was The Mid Surrey Squash Club, just opposite our house where he became quite a celebrity and many members' stories are contained in my book.

The best thing that happened to Joe, apart from meeting me, was marrying Pam who first persuaded Jane Fonda to rent Hill House to him she being wary of rock & rollers.

Throughout these years I was not aware of his extreme use of drugs and alcohol although there had been signs e.g. when Joe was quite ill I did take him for a full check up in Harley Street with Dr. Nabarro whose diagnosis was that if Joe did not severely reduce his consumption of alcohol he did not reckon he had long to live, or words to that effect. Well Joe did take note and to some extent followed this advice, laying off the spirits and preferring lager. When last I saw Joe after his gig at The Tower of London in 2005 he had given up alcohol and cigarettes and was looking good.

A delightful side effect of writing the book, Sue nee Bunning, who was one of those I contacted, joined me for lunch on 23rd December 2014

Bernard Pendry

after 33 years apart and on 23 January 2017 we married.

Could write so much more as these were magical times. never experienced before or since. For mote information read by book MY MEMORIES OF JOE.

According to Ray Charles, Joe was the greatest white soul singer of all time.

ARRIVING IN NEW ORLEANS

JOE IN OUR KITCHEN

*WELL INEBRIATED AFTER
MEETING WITH A&M RECORDS*

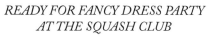

*READY FOR FANCY DRESS PARTY
AT THE SQUASH CLUB*

Bernard Pendry

WITH WIFE PAM
AT THEIR RANCH

FAMILY CANOEING AT
JANE FONDA'S RANCH

JOE'S NEW BARN

JOE'S ATTEMPT AT
GOLF. DRIVEN MY MARK.

SEE OUR BUDGERIGAR ON HIS SHOULDER

SUNSET MARQUIS

CHAPTER 23

THE GOLF CLUB GREAT BRITAIN

My only original idea

From the other chapters you will see I had been a member of Leatherhead Golf Club for 26 years when the whole ethos of the club changed causing me to resign.

Without being a member of a golf club I contacted the English Golf Union (EGU), the controlling body of amateur golf, to enquire how I could preserve my handicap. Quite a demonstrative answer, "no way if you're not a member of a club affiliated to them". It struck me as being equitably and morally wrong; everyone should have the ability to have a handicap.

This sowed the seed for me to consider what could be done. Why should the EGU be the only ones to control handicaps? So in 1986 I launched THE GOLF CLUB OF GREAT BRITAIN with the idea of making handicaps available to all and employed June Conboy and Lynn to help promote it with adverts in the golfing press. Peter Allis, the doyen of the world of golf, had seen the adverts and invited me to his house in Hindhead, Surrey to chat over my ideas. He shared my philosophy that all golfers should have the ability to earn a handicap whether or not they are members of a golf club and he agreed to be our President. In the course of his commentating and articles he often gave us a mention.

We organised monthly tournaments, overseas trips, long weekends tournaments and slowly it got off the ground. One early member, Gary Jackson, was a senior vice president of a large American company, attended one of our weekend events where he befriended Sally a new member who was there on her own. A romance followed and not long after they married. It was he who arranged an annual trip to Arizona at very reasonable rates helped by having executive dealing with British Airways. He was also the one who developed our own handicapping system based on that used by the EGU.

I was not prepared to invest large sums of money as I had seen others try to launch other golf related ideas, notably someone had talked Tony Jacklin, the famous English professional and Ryder Cup Captain into launching the TONY JACKLIN CLUB offering to award official handicaps and invested £250,000. It didn't take long before they came up against the EGU who flatly refused to accept their handicaps. So it crumbled. We never indicated that our system complied with the EGU rules.

I had always been on friendly terms with the EGU` informing them of everything we were doing. Sometime in the mid nineties their secretary invited me to their head office in Woodhall Spa, Lincolnshire, as there was something he wanted to discuss. After showing me around this magnificent complex with everything a golfer could desire he let me know the reason. The EGU were going to launch their own handicapping scheme for golfers who were not members of a club, which of course would be in competition with the GCGB. I asked whether these handicaps would qualify for their national tournaments and was not surprised that they admitted they would not. I thanked him and wished them well. With a substantial budget they launched the scheme via GOLF ENGLAND. It was not a success.

A surprising thing was the number of overseas members joining from around the world most notably Germany. Apparently private clubs in those countries required a handicap certificate to be able to play their courses. These new members confirmed that they encountered no problems when presenting their GCGB handicaps. But thinking to the future I launched THE INTERNATIONAL GOLFER CLUB for all overseas golfers, which seems to work.

You will note the word 'OF' in the title. Seven years after the launch someone else starts operating under the same name so I made a complaint to the Trading Standards people. The results were that the others had to stop operating and we had to delete the "OF" as it inferred we were the predominant club in GB.

The Clubs jogged along and 34 years later it is still going, now run by Kate Brown who bought the business in 2006.

GOLF GROUP. GCGB

OUR ABODE WHEN OPENING A GOLF COURSE IN ITALY

PETER ALLIS THE GOLF DOYEN

Bernard Pendry

CHAPTER 24

PETS

Everyone loves a pet and here are the stories of those that came into my life.

FLUFF *the cat*

This was when I was a young boy and Fluff roamed the house as he pleased. He (maybe a she, who knows?) was big and sported a bushy white coat, Mum always complaining about the fur balls he choked up. Anyway he was not paid much attention and one day I asked Mum if she had seen him to which she replied "I had him put down about two months ago". What a sad end.

BOBBY *the blue budgerigar*

Bobby was the most adorable pet anyone could ever have, he (or maybe she!) was one of the family and had free reign of the large kitchen/dining room. At meal times he would join us by sitting on anyone's shoulder and eat peas or anything any of us held in our mouth. He seemed to really like all of us and we adored him.

Then for some reason he contracted *bumble foot* a horrid complaint that affected his ability to stand on his perch. It gradually got worse ending in his death. We, that is Nicola, Mark, Michael and I were in mourning, we dug a grave in the garden and laid him to rest in a nice wooden box. Many tears were shed.

NIBBLES *Nicola's and* SPURS *Michael's rabbits*

One of them was a victim of a fox but the survivor Nibbles lived happily in the pen and hutch erected in the garden going hopety, hopety hop. I think it was a neighbour who asked if we could look after her rabbit for a while and brought round her rabbit in a pen and he (she?) went hopety, hopety hop. I thought why not let them go hopety, hopety hop together, wouldn't it be fun. So I lifted her rabbit and put it in with NIBBLES. Well my expectation of a friendly get together was shattered, they went at each other like warring gladiators, before I could get to them they had disappeared into the hutch, the noise was horrendous. The entrance was too small to get a hand in so I had to pull the roof off, grab this huge ball of flying fur and pull them apart never letting them share a pen again.

SHANDY *the Hamster*

Shandy the hamster roamed the house as he wanted and it was basically Nicola who tended him. One day someone asked where Shandy was, nobody knew and then discovered no one had seen him for weeks. More weeks went by and the only explanation seemed to be he must have escaped or died. A month later he appeared from a floorboard looking emaciated but otherwise OK.

SHERRY *the Springer spaniel*

When Pam came back into my life it was a case of *have me have my dog*. Sherry had been a present from customers when she ran The Hop Bag Pub in Farnham and it was definitely her dog and no one else's, hence she was not a favourite of the family. I got on with her OK but on one occasion when visiting Richmond Park, Sherry was in the open boot while Pam went for ice creams, so I tried to coax Sherry out, she didn't move so I reached in and quickly retracted when Sherry bared her teeth and growled. When Pam came back I told her to be careful, she just reached in, grabbed Sherry by the collar and yanked her out. The best thing about Sherry was she was a marvelous swimmer and would swim for ages.

Her end was sad. She was a ripe old age, a bit incontinent, didn't like going for walks preferring to just lay there giving the impression she had given up. Pam made the heart wrenching decision to have her put down and arranged for the vet to visit. Sherry was asleep in the kitchen when there was a knock on the front door, we knew it would be the vet and were astonished and troubled when Sherry got up and walked to the door. Had Pam been too hasty but she saw it through.

A BLACK & WHITE SPRINGER SPANIEL

After Sherry had gone we decided no more dogs. Taking Mum in her wheelchair for a walk in Bishops Park we got chatting to a young lady walking a beautiful Springer Spaniel and discovered that she was walking the dog for an elderly man who lived in Gowan Avenue, (the road where Jill Dando was murdered in 1999) and because he was incapable of walking his dog was seeking someone he could give it to. Pam's ears pricked up, we took the gentleman's number, visited him and agreed to take the dog, and he refused to take any money, just wanted caring owners.

On the way home we called into Richmond Park and what joy it was to see him race all over the place. At this stage we had two cats, Floyd & Sox and did not think there would be a problem but as soon as we got inside the dog flew at the cats, Floyd whizzed out through the cat flap, Sox jumped on the table, presumably thinking he would be safe but the dog reared up and got Sox in his jaws pulling him to the floor, no doubt playfully, but to us it was a horror. No harm was done except it was obvious the dog didn't get on with cats so it was a return journey.

BENJI *Eileen & Rays Cocker Spaniel*

Eileen & Ray were staying with us one Christmas with Benji a very nice dog. There was a knock on the door and Pam opened the door to Win who walked straight past her "Benji what a lovely surprise" not even bothering to turn round and say hello to Pam. Surely dogs should not get in the way of social graces!

OTHER ANIMALS

Michael had numerous creatures, snakes, lizards, spiders, geckos etc. All we have now are Koi carp.

CHAPTER 25

THE EFFECTS OF LOCKDOWN

At February 2021

Nobody saw Coronavirus, known as Covid 19, coming so we were all unprepared for what lay ahead.

Soon it was necessary for the government to take drastic action and they had the dilemma, the two huge questions being what is more important (a) to give priority to the National Health Service to minimize deaths and (b) save the economy which was suffering big time with the closure of a vast number of businesses and organisations, the stock markets around the world have plummeted causing shareholders to lose billions. It is now mid May 2020 and there is no clear way ahead.

As far as Sue & I are concerned there are no vital changes unless you consider the reduction in our wealth, however golf courses and croquet clubs are closed so we set up a four hoop croquet game on our lawn, with a set of balls borrowed from the club and I erected a curtain made of snooker table cloth taken from the RAC when the tables were recovered into which I endlessly chip and pitch golf balls. Then we regularly cycle our electric bikes over every green space within 5 miles notably Ashtead & Epsom Commons and Princes Coverts.

Both daughter Nicola and Son Mike caught the virus, suffered for two weeks but thankfully recovered and now immune, or so they think.

ZOOM has come into its own; meet ups with the family, poker with the usual family and friends where I regularly lose but so enjoyable chatting.

Bernard Pendry

We do abide by the social distancing advice, which is fun when we have members of the family round all spaced out around the garden.

As someone said "it is like a war but this time we are on the same side'

How long this is going to go on is a mystery but hopefully when you read this everything will be back to a new form of normal.

Latest personal development 16th March 2021.

I had befriended an old lady, Margaret, who lived on her own in a West Country village, a neighbour of my son and daughter-in-law. I had heard how confused she was and couldn't remember anything. I got chatting to her and found her fascinating recounting stories of being a leading ballerina and then a nurse and how at age 40 marrying but this brought tears as he had passed away only a few weeks ago. Being only two years younger than her I told her how to improve her short term memory and gave her a note book advising that she write down daily anything that had happened like phone calls, visitors and noting anything that crossed her mind.

She asked if I would help her with the things that sprung to mind but I said I could only help if her stepson, Adrian and Jayne her social worker approved. She said she would phone them and I left. Within a few minutes I received a phone call from someone at the Social Services, not Jayne, warning that I should have nothing to do with Margaret and would not listen to anything I had to say. The call ended with her threatening to call the police. Mulling over the situation I returned the call, but a different lady answered to whom I explained what had happened and confirming I would totally withdraw from the case. Case closed although I did feel guilty abandoning Margaret.

Today I get a phone call from my son, the police are there questioning them and Margaret about breaking Lockdown rules and wanting to know who I am. So at present I am awaiting a knock on the door. Anyone found guilty could face a £10,000 fine.

CHAPTER 26

FINANCE AND MONEY

Right from a young age I worked to earn money (Chapter 4) and when I started work age 17 I earned £300 p.a. rising to £1,100 p.a. when in 1959 I became a chartered accountant. Then at South Bank Estates my salary rose to £4,500 by 1970 when I left.

None of this was very exciting but it permitted a reasonable life style, mortgages, cars, holidays of the package type in the Mediterranean and later to The States.

The big change came when I became a partner in Nabarros and my income increased year by year, nothing huge but money to spare and this is when I started saving and investing in pensions. Don't let anyone put you off pensions; they are a lifeline to a relaxed retirement.

Investing in property can rarely go wrong and every house I bought always sold for substantially more. I wish I had investigated in buying properties to rent because in days gone bye it was possible to buy with a mortgage, the rents covering the interest payments. Maybe I could have been a millionaire!

The best financial move I made was investing in properties other than residences. First I bought 124 Ewell Road, Surbiton for another office. None of the other partners were interested so I raised the mortgage. This was sold for a handsome profit in 1980 when I bought 300/301 Ewell Road, Surbiton. Again none of the partners were interested so I raised a huge bank mortgage the interest rate being 8.5%. When I learnt there were lower interest rates available I contacted the bank manager complaining. He said "Bernard I can lower the rate but at present you have a fixed interest mortgage so this would be changed to a variable". I said I would let him know and thinking about it decided not to change.

Bernard Pendry

Thank goodness I didn't because not long after interest rates spiraled to 17%. Had I changed I don't know what would have happened. I had set up The Pendry Trust and bought number 300 in the Trust.

The Pendry Trust came in very useful because every year I paid the rents to all the grandchildren and claimed back the tax paid. This went on until the property was sold. So now the Trust had substantial funds and over the years I made sizable gifts to various members of the family when needed.

This latest acquisition was for part office but mainly for letting and I had fabulous tenants in the name of Barrelfield who took every space when available including when I closed the office. When they considered moving to larger offices I made them an offer to reduce all rents. They stayed for another few years but when they finally moved to a new office and warehouse on the Brooklands Estate in about 1990, I put the offices up for sale. I had no idea of their worth and it took some time to find a buyer but eventually sold them for £590,000 divided between me and the Trust, enough to pay off the mortgage and leave me with a nice few pennies. This was when I started investing in stocks & shares. It still amazes me how their values continually raise.

I had bought, in Pam's name, a beachside town house, Macarena C, in Calahonda, Spain for 9000 pesetas, which was to be a family holiday home for many years. When Pam died the property passed to our five children who rented it out but the Spanish rental laws changed for the worse so in 2018 they sold it for 250,000 euros. This was fortuitous because in early 2020 the Coronavirus virus struck which put property prices in a spin, especially Spanish rental properties exacerbated when travel was severely restricted.

I had purchased a peculiar old run down coach house in the back streets of Tolworth with the idea of kitting it out for storage. Access was by a road between two blocks of flats. Another purchase the other partners were not interested in. A couple of years went by and I had done nothing with it so I decided to put it on the market. I did get a good offer that I accepted but the buyer's solicitor raised the point that according to the legal document I had no access rights to the property. He was right so the big question was "why didn't my solicitor discover this when I bought it? The deal fell through so I considered suing and discussions followed. After some time my solicitor discovered that the original access road was from the rear over which the flat owners had built a block of garages. So now what? The owners were a Resident's Association and no one wanted to take responsibility and it wasn't until we started legal proceedings that they signed a document giving us rights of access. Now the property was put back on the marked and fortunately for my solicitor it was a higher price.

When I moved from 30 Ruxley Lane I bought 14 Lady Forsdyke Way, Epsom in Pam and my joint names for £545,000 thinking we would live here forever. Tragically Pam died in 2013 and by her will that I had drawn up, her half went to our five children. No problem whatsoever that was until Sue came back into my life and was now my main financial concern so I wanted to be able to leave the property to her. The five were amenable to transfer their share to me on the promise they would each receive £20,000 on my death.

I did not sell Ruxley Lane but profitably rented it out for a few years to extremely helpful tenants. For personal reasons they left so what should I do? I did put it on the market but never received an acceptable offer. Laying in bed one morning I thought "why do I want to sell, this is like a family home?" And there and then decided to do a deal with the five children, I would transfer the ownership to them and in return they would pay me a monthly sum of £1,300. This is still in existence slightly altered.

Unforeseen windfall. When The Royal Automobile Club sold its interest in its motoring service, every member got £34,000. We never saw this coming but it did raise the question "presumably the price depended on profitability so what had happened to these profits in the past?"

All in all I am contented, never aiming to be a millionnaire

Bernard Pendry

CHAPTER 27

A SELECTION OF HOLIDAYS

I have always prided myself in arranging yearly holidays for family and friends first to package holidays around the Mediterranean then further afield and more costly. Obviously I could fill up another book but here are a few that may be of interest for one reason or another.

FIRST SKIING HOLIDAY

Up until age 40 there had only been summer holidays but friends from Kent talked me into making up a party of 16 for two weeks in Sauze d'Oulx, Italy. I had no idea how to ski so booked in for lessons at Esher Dry Ski School, Surrey. It soon became obvious that my legs would not go into a snowplough position so I had to attempt just parallel turns to slow down and even then it was difficult. But so what?

On arriving at the resort the party was made up of 7 accomplished skiers, 7 relative beginners and two about OK. Us beginners booked into a ski school and first lesson was side stepping up a slope about 30 yards then snow ploughing down so they could sort out the absolute beginners. Me not being able to snow plough attempted at parallel skiing must have impressed the instructors because when they allotted each to a group I was not in the beginner's class.

My group was lead by a German lady who marched us to a chair lift for a ride half way up the slopes. She ignored my pleas that I had never been skiing or on a chair lift and basically said "get on". While I enjoyed the ride I had no idea how to get off but the person with me just said lean forward and push so I alighted just in time not to be hit my the following chair.

Now we all stood on this raised area with a narrow path going down with a sharp bend about four meters further. Off went the rest of the group but I stood there totally confused until the German lady yelled "get down here we are waiting". Nervously I set off but when I got to the turn I had no idea how to navigate it so went straight on into a heap of snow. Trying to extricate my skis buried in the deep snow took ages and all the while I was conscious of what the others must be thinking. Of course eventually I did join the group and off we went. I later learnt this was a blue route so was manageable.

During the holiday I became quite proficient and fancied my chances when I organised a last day race. It was to be a pairs race, a proficient skier pared with a beginner and the two OK, starting from the top after lunch. The morning was my last lesson and I was prepared to hone my skills until some stupid member of the group cut right across me, I fell badly damaging a shoulder so ended my dream of being a winner. The rest thought it was great fun.

Sauze d'Oulx is like Southend, Essex, everyone having fun and the bars well used. The famous bar there is The Andy Cap Bar.

KENYA JULY 1985

I really splashed out on this three weeks holiday. Plus Pam there was Nicola and her friend Sara, Mike and his then girlfriend Dawn.

Met at Nairobi Airport by Emmanuel who was to be our driver of a large people carrier for the safari part of the holiday. He was a really nice guy and we all took it in turns to sit with him, but as the days went on the armpits of his green shirt became more and more stained ending with no one wanting to get too close. But so what?

First stop was Lake Nakuru and on the way we saw our first animal, a lone gnu peering out of bushes only later to see massive herds of them. The lake was surrounded by wading flamingoes who when we got too close took off in a cloud of pink feathers.

At Ambroseli Reserve we had a wonderful chalet, a short walk from the main area with a swimming pool. One evening after dining we arrived at the chalet and there was a very large grasshopper buzzing about. The ladies were a bit concerned and after shooing it away opened the door making a dash inside to the bathroom and slamming the door, but the grasshopper was quicker and had beat them to it. There were lots of squealing and shouting as though they were being tortured. It finally ceased when the poor thing ended in the toilet. We men freed it.

It was hear we learnt of the jungle messages that went between the guides when Emanuel got a message that a lion had gone from the pride with a lioness to mate. We drove to the spot and there they were, Emanuel explaining he would mount her for about 20 seconds, roll over while she would lay on her back with her legs in the air, wait for 20 minutes and start all over again this going on for hours. They were totally unconcerned of our presence. He further explained that after a day or two of this the pair would return to the pride, he staying some distance away while she would go to the pride to be fated by all. The lionesses would go off and make a kill and when ready he would saunter down and choose the best bits. How male dominated!

Next day the message was an elephantess being wooed. We drove through a herd of 46 elephants and in a clearing she swaying from side to side surrounded four bulls also swaying. Emanuel explained that the bulls were waiting for her to make up her mind which one she wanted to mate with. Well we were there for over an hour but she was still swaying so were the males.

On the way back we came across a huge python with its kill, a large antelope with impressive long horns. The snake kept going round the antelope opening its mouth trying to reach the top of the horns. Again we watched this for over an hour but the python could not manage and sloped off. Emanuel explained that now the scavengers would arrive and within an hour there would just be fragments of the carcass left.

After a few nights at Tsavo Reserve watching a variety of animals drinking in the nearby lake we headed for Mombasa where there were street traders all over the place. Our Naili Beach Hotel was right on the banks of the Indian Ocean and a short way away was Melindi Beach the most wonderful place for snorkeling, the variety of fish far outshone Australia's barrier reefs.

At this hotel they prompted us to play volleyball. I had never played the game but joined in and soon it was obvious the teams were playing to win. The guy next to me was so aggressive, diving all over the place. I can't remember who won but I got chatting to the guy who turned out to be Martin Edward the chairman of Manchester United football club. While chatting to him his son was teaching his mother how to windsurf. She was up and down but eventually caught a wind and off she set, straight out to sea with her son yelling, "fall off" to no effect. He set off swimming fast and managed to catch her.

Son Mike always had a wish to go deep-sea fishing so I arranged a trip. It was a rickety boat moored just up the river mouth and with two other passengers off we sailed. No problem, out of the river into a sheltered sea but when we cleared a reef the sea was rough and it wasn't long before the up & down, up & down made me violently sea sick, I tried the loo but the toilet roll was soaked, back on deck I clung to a post retching over the side. The 'captain' was worried and suggested we return straight away but not wanting to spoil the others trip I hung on. Eventually we got back and I just flopped on the bed and passed out.

Back to Nairobi by night train and home.

EGYPT

Pam and I had seen this travel programme on Egypt and thought 'why not'. So we booked a two-week guided tour starting in a luxury hotel in Cairo a busy bustling city. A trip to the local market was astounding, about a mile long with side lanes off each side packed with shops and stalls selling everything imaginable. Even more amazing was a trip to the Museum where a whole floor housed the contents removed from Tutankhamen's tomb including statues, gold jewellery, his Mummy, chariots, model boats, canonic jars, gilded furniture and more presumably removed by Howard Carter after he discovered the tomb in November 1922. I assumed it must have been a huge tomb but later when we visited in was just two fairly small rooms.

Always being fascinated by pyramids we took a taxi ride to Giza Pyramid thinking it would be mystically in the desert. Not so, the city had expanded over the years so it was just in a suburb and sat there as a huge pile of bricks. The way in was down a square tunnel that you had to bend almost double to waddle down with your nose up someone's arse to the centre and after this all that was there was a bare stone plinth that the guide informed us that was where the Mummy used to be. The walls were totally bare and disappointing. Just outside was the massive Sphinx, impressive except for the loss of its nose that had been blasted off by Italian soldiers on the orders of Napoleon in 1789.

We were due to leave the next day for a flight to Abu Simbel. That night we had booked for a gala dinner in the hotel and we danced to the early hours. Returning to our room there was a message; we had to leave the hotel by 6 a.m. for the flight. I was furious, I needed my 8 hours sleep so I sent a note to the organiser that there was no way we could make it. They arranged a later flight but it meant we missed the onward flight to Abu Simbel Temple. What a thing to miss just for a few hours sleep. The temple was built by Ramesses ll and the whole structure that displayed large effigies of four pharaohs had been moved here to allow the Aswan Dam to be built across the Nile.

We did get to Luxor where we joined a cruise ship where they divided us into groups of ten for the various tours and a Group leader had to be nominated. Our group was comprised of eight Americans and us who all insisted I be the Leader. We got on so well it was fun all the way. They thought it humorous when in a market I was negotiating with a trader to buy a nightshirt and instead of beating him down said his prices were too cheap and settled for more.

It was from here that we visited The Valley of the Kings, truly wonderful with every tomb highly festooned with colourful murals as though they were painted yesterday, truly the highlight of the holiday.

Sailing up the Nile was so peaceful, we docked at Luxor just for a break and as it was right on the banks of the Nile I decided to go for a swim, Pam warned me of the crocodiles but I informed her there were none since the building of the Aswan Dam. However I couldn't stop thinking there may be a rogue one who escaped.

It ended with a gala night on board and everyone saying "we must meet again" of course never thinking anyone would. We would gladly welcome the American so it was a great surprise at the dismissive receptions from two couples we called on in California, expecting a warm welcome like 'how nice to see you, come in for a drink' instead a handshake and a couple of minutes chat.

Xxxxxxxxxxxxx

Enough of this it sounds like a travelogue so just some short snippets.

Took son Mike for a week in **LAS VEGAS**, Hotel Bellagio, open top Ford Mustang, ride out to The Grand Canyon where Mike was spellbound and could have stopped there all day. On the drive there in the middle of a desert an old speed cop appeared from nowhere to inform us we were speeding. Nice old boy, no ticket.

Xxxxxxxxxxxxx

My 80th took all the family, 28 in all, to a **Manor House near Chichester,** Sussex. A long weekend of games, singing, cooking (self catering), rifle shooting won by Sue. It was a fabulous holiday marred only by the owner, who had walked me round to inspect before we left, to then send an email accusing us of leaving the place in a mess. I think he was annoyed because son-in-law Neil had beaten him in his own squash courts.

Xxxxxxxxxxxxx

At the end of one of our holidays at Joe Cockers, Pam and I took an internal flight to **Syracuse, New York State** (bloody expensive, I think we could have flown home for the price). We stayed with friends who showed us the area. So like England countryside. If the Queen ever banishes me this is where I want to go.

Xxxxxxxxxxxxx

New York. After a carriage ride around Central Park Pam and I dined atop the Twin Towers admiring the fantastic views. So tragic.

Xxxxxxxxxxxxxx

Croquet tour. Being keen croqueteers Sue & I decided to forgo a foreign holiday and went on a tour of croquet clubs along the south coast with our electric bikes on the back staying for a night or two in hotels. Hempworth C.C. in The New Forest, Sidmouth C.C. on the sea front, Budleigh Salterton C.C. premium club with 13 lawns, Cornwall C.C. tucked away in the hills where Sue found a toad in one on the holes (Toad in the Hole) and last but the best Bath C.C. where we parked the car unloaded the bikes and cycled into the city before cycling the 13 mile circuitous route along the river and canal banks. Fortunately the weather was kind.

Xxxxxxxxxxxxxx

New Zealand. Sue and I splash out a bit of money. Business class flight to Sydney, boarded a cruise ship, lovely views of their famous opera house, over night to Melbourne for a day and then off to New Zealand's southern tip marveling at the fjords while the ship cruise between towering cliffs. Some places of particular interest, The National Museum of New Zealand in **Wellington** with the history of the Maori nation. **Auckland** and *The America's Cup Village. The Waipoura Forest* where a Maori leader told me how the kauri trees are inter-twinned with their history. These are huge trees, which covered most of their land until they have been decimated for buildings. A recreation of the *home of the Hobbits* as seen in the movie. **Queenstown** the city for fun, exhilarating jet boat ride hurling between rocks on the Shotover River. **Bay of Islands** where the British and Maori signed the treaty, sail through the Hole in the Rock, squeeze in tight!

Xxxxxxxxxxxxxx

Australia with Pam. Travelled the west coast from Melbourne to Port Douglas from where we took a sailing ship to the The Great Barrier Reef. This was amazing for various reasons, first we set sail passing many islands which soon disappeared and all you could sea was ocean, then a pontoon appeared where we alighted to be met my helpers who kitted us out with masks and flippers and into the ocean we went to be surrounded by an array of brightly coloured fish. The coral was beautiful some just below the surface then descending into the depths. We did win a few dollars in Cairns Casino. Australia is a wonderful place (at least the small part we saw).

Xxxxxxxxxxxxx

Australia with Sue. Someone advertised a croquet tour to Adelaide to compete against local clubs; this was something not to be missed. Before arriving in Adelaide we spent a week in Freemantle and expecting the weather to be hot and sunny we pack no warm clothes. How unfortunate, the weather was cold and wet. While here we took a trip to Rottnest Island a typical holiday resort famous for the rare Quokkas, cute little animals with rat like tails. Flight to Adelaide and after playing 6 clubs, winning two losing four, we sailed to Kangaroo Island another attractive holiday resort.

Xxxxxxxxxxxxx

Cruise of the north Mediterranean coasts with Viking Ocean Cruises

Of course, first class cabin for Sue and me starting from Barcelona. If you ever go to stay make sure it is in Los Ramblas, a wide pedestrian thoroughfare from the Med through the middle of the city which is quite action packed.

Nine destinations all so memorable but those that have special memories are:

Monte Carlo, the spectacular casino, the most amazing and largest Oceanographic Museum in the world just the richness of the place.

Florence, The Leaning Tower of Pisa, amazing it doesn't fall over.

Rome. You could spend a week here and not see everything. The

Colosseum, Pompeii the world as it was 2000 years ago, The Trevi Fountain, throw in a coin and make a wish.

Dubrovnik a preserved medieval city that Bernard Shaw called 'Paradise on Earth'. Panoramic views from the mountains are spectacular.

Split, Croatia. It was in the mountains that we hire a Doon buggy that Sue drove over some treacherous ground. It was while in the mountain that we saw the remains of the fortifications built in the 1990s for their war of independence against Yugoslavia.

And finally

Venice, the wonder of the Doge's Palace, the gondolas, so busy they hardly moved, St. Mark's Square for a coffee if you could accept the price!

Xxxxxxxxxxxxxx

APPENDECIES

APPENDIX 1

OUR GRANDAD: A WOULD BE GOLFER

I'm David age 17 and I'm Eddie age 18, two of Granddad's 14 grandchildren. Granddad has told us so many stories about his golfing life we thought we would put him to the test. So we contrived to meet with him one fine summers day in his secluded garden listening to the flow of water from the fountain into the Koi carp pond.

We already knew Granddad was born in 1936, had 3 children and loved golf. So here goes with the questions.

Q. Granddad when did you start playing golf and where?

A. My introduction to golf was in 1948 age 12 when my Dad took me to Richmond Park Golf Complex. I'd like to say I took to it like a duck to water but unfortunately that was a long way from reality. However it did kindle an interest and I started to enjoy reading books about the technique and history of the game.

Q. You talk a lot about your Dad, what sort of golfer was he?

A. Possibly the worst golfer who ever lived. He didn't take up the game until well into his 40s. never had a lesson, never read any books on the game so basically never had a clue. To him 3 putting was a bonus and only once in his life did he beat 100. All his golf was at Richmond Park or the occasional day out with The Association of Electrical Engineers Golf Society, of which he was a founder, where his claim to fame was winning more wooden spoons than anyone in history.

Bernard Pendry

He did have one rather unusual hole in one. In those days woods were wood and for fun I had sanded one down, an old persimmon driver, painted it gloss white and presented it to Dad. He thought it was terrific and it became his pride and joy. On a cold and frosty morning off he went with his cronies. On the 2nd hole of the Dukes course, a short par 3, there was a temporary green and forward mat tee making it about 90 yards. Out came the white beauty, whollop, topped it bounced down the icy fairway and miraculously disappeared into the hole. He was so thrilled that next day off he set for the office of The Hole in One Golf Society in Croydon. When asked to produce the scorecard, Dad enquired whether it was absolutely necessary. Naturally the reply was "it is customary and why wouldn't you want us to see it?" Sheepishly Dad replied "well I took a 13 on the next hole". He did come away with the tie that became a prize possession shown off at every opportunity.

Q. So you liked playing with your Dad?

A. You must be joking, he was the most infuriating person to play with. He invariably said "good shot" no matter whether is was good, bad or indifferent. Never took much interest in who was doing what. To his credit he really only played the game for the exercise and thoroughly enjoyed it. On one occasion we were playing against his friend Charlie Oliver and his son, Chris who was a few years younger than me. I played reasonably well and got us to the 18th one up. Dad was getting one of his many shots and some how got to within 18 inches of the hole for 4 net 3. All he had to do was sink the putt and we won the match. It was easier to get than miss but miss he did remarking, "it's much better to halve than win". I was so irritated that I tossed my ball into the air and, baseball style, smashed it into the middle of the park with my putter. All was forgotten over a drink in the 19th but on my next game I got to the first green, addressed my putt to discover that the head was at right angles to the shaft. Lesson, never use a golf club for baseball.

Q. You talk lovingly about Richmond Park. What was it really like?

A. Oh! Happy days, young, full of energy and enthusiasm.

The golf complex was one of the best municipal set-ups in the south. Two excellent courses, The Princes up the hill and The Dukes down. I didn't play much in my early teens, just the odd game with school mates then at 17 I joined The Putney Park Golf Society one of three societies that used Richmond Park as their club. Then it was golf every Saturday morning, hoping to tee off around 8.30 to 9.00 in either a competition or a friendly. In this day and age with so much golf on offer, it is difficult to comprehend what had to be done to get an early start time. Queuing started at 6 o'clock, maybe earlier. I was lucky because I had teamed up with Sully and old boy (although I doubt he was as old as I am now) who was an early riser and always got us a good time. I can still see him now, pipe in mouth, humming some indistinguishable tune, jangling coins or keys in his pocket while contemplating his next shot.

The only time I beat Sully to the queue was when brother-in-law Ray and I went there straight from an all night party.

Q. Did you ever win anything?

A. Only once at PPGS to get my name on an honours board. I always pointed it out with pride but you can't see it now as the clubhouse burnt down a few years ago.

Then once at Leatherhead in 1982 winning the annual Knock Out competition known as The Ladies Challenge. Again once at The Royal Automobile Club when I won The Captains prize and you can see my name on the honours board in 2007.

Q. So why did you stop playing at Richmond Park?

A. In 1957 a few of my close playing friends, Keith Drayton, Mac, the three Clack brothers, left and joined the Royal Wimbledon Artisans. They asked me to join them and said they would get me a dodgy address to conform to the rules of artisanship. I considered it but being half way in my studies for a chartered accountant, I decided it would not be appropriate. They were great characters, Dennis Clack, 5 feet 4 playing off 4 handicap, who regularly won the club championship. I

Bernard Pendry

remember once playing with him and on the 10th tee he was addressing the ball, when a motorbike, presumably with no silencer, went roaring past on the main A3, not 100 yards away. His tee shot was immaculate. To me that noise would have put me right off but when I enquired of Dennis he said, "I heard something but it didn't affect my swing". Keith and his wife, Joan, became god parents to son Mark, Mac the scoundrel who was a law unto himself who illegally tripped their electric meter, his wife moved something nearby, BANG and she got thrown across the floor, Andy Jess who played cack handed but was a good 9 handicapper and could putt on any green no matter how rough, Charlie Hanniford the gentleman's hairdresser at Harrods, always immaculately dressed and many others whose names have faded with time. If you get to visit the clubhouse in Richmond Park you will see my name on the PPGC board around about the late 50s. (Oops, no you won't, the clubhouse burnt down).

About this time I was playing regular squash and one of the guys, John Upton, asked if I would like to join Leatherhead Golf Club where he was a member. Like my Dad I had never contemplated joining a private club but gave it a try and never regretted joining in 1959.

Q. What are artisans?

A. In the early days of golf, in fact right up until the 1950s, golf was a game for the upper classes and comparatively expensive. It was also a case of "the old boys network'; unless you were proposed and seconded by a member you hadn't a chance of getting in. To placate the local traders they were allowed to join a separate section, the artisans, and for a modest annual fee they could play early mornings and evenings provided they did some menial works on the course like repairing pitch marks, raking bunkers and the like. Only a few clubs continue this scheme, the reason I suspect being that many traders are more wealthy than bankers, solicitors etc. Be wary when playing an artisan, they are most dedicated golfers and a force to be reckoned with, so competitive.

Q. Were you any good at this stage?

A. Not really, I could hit a ball a long way but never quite certain which way it would go. As I said, I read many books, developed a good full swing, and was reasonably proficient on the putting green but useless at chipping and pitching. I did get my handicap down to 12 but my dream of reaching single figures never materialized.

Q. Why didn't you have lessons?

A. I did. When I was 18, Keith Drayton and I went for an hour's lesson with Bill Cox, a tubby little man, at Fulwell Golf Club. In his day he was the doyen of golf, a cross between Peter Alliss and John Jacobs. He gave us a good work out and at the end gave us an honest summing up. He told Keith, a big strong fellow, that with practice he could be a reasonable golfer. To me he said, "Bernard, if you do not find a way to strengthen you wrists, you will never be a good golfer", "Idiot" I thought but he has been proved right.

Another most memorable lesson was when your uncle, Michael, was working for a season at La Manga Club in Spain. I had gone down with daughter Nicola, for a week. When I learnt that the resident pro was Vicente Ballesteros, older brother of Seve, so I couldn't resist booking a lesson. He is a very big man and the main theme of his teaching was to instill the use of the wrists in generating club head speed. He got me to address the ball, stood to my left, leaned over engulfing both my hands with his huge right hand and proceeded to whizz my hands and the club back and through a dozen or so times. I felt like a rag doll but it did instill me with how to generate club head speed, hence I have always been able to hit a reasonable long ball.

Q. Tell us a little about your time at Leatherhead.

A. I was a member for 26 years from 1959 to 1985 and most of it was very enjoyable. With regular partner, John Harris, we played every Saturday pitting our skills against a variety of opponents. The après golf in the 19th was always full of good humour plus the occasional game of snooker or game of 3-card brag. Over the years I did reduce my handicap from 18 to 12 but only succeeded in getting my name on one honour board and that was for winning the annual knock out competition. This time the clubhouse has not burnt down so you can still point out my name to your friends.

Every year they held a selling sweep. The idea was that after a dinner and much wine names were drawn out of a hat and paired up. They were then auctioned and went to the highest bidder. I had resisted the temptation to attend for many years, wary of the high gamblers in those days but I relented and attended in 1976. What a jolly affair and when the pairs went up for auction many hundreds were bid especially for known golfers. Out of the hat came The Baron paired with The Vicar. I didn't know them personally but knew they had a reputation, I thought for golf, but obviously wrong. The bidding went £60, £80, £100 £120. It was going so rapidly I could see it breaking the £200 barrier so just for fun I bid £140 and waited expectantly for the next bid. It went quiet and they were knocked down to me. I was flabbergasted but at least under the rules they were allowed to buy half of themselves, which would save me £70. No such luck, they didn't want any part of themselves. Wouldn't it be a fabulous story if they went on to win. Sadly there was no fairy tale ending.

On the day of the Selling Sweep son Michael, was caddying for me. A rare occasion but at age 12 well able to pull my trolley. All was going well although it had come on to rain so brollies up. On the tee of the par 5 8th hole my drive was sliced and heading for the trees. I turned to Michael to shout "can you see it?" but before I could utter a word he said "Mary Poppins" standing there raising and lowering the brolley, quite oblivious of me even having hit the drive. Much mirth to all except me.

Michael's sense of "fun" hasn't diminished over the years. Some years later we were playing on the same 8th hole. The course was busy and plays very slow. The four ball behind had waited every shot, as had we. Approaching my drive, a good one down the middle, a ball flew over my head. I was furious and turned to shout a variety of obscenities when Michael, with a grin, owned up to having tossed it over my head. I didn't know whether to laugh or strangle him.

Q. Leatherhead seems ideal. Why did you leave?

A. A combination of things. In the early days it was run very much like a members club, although in fact it was owned by shareholders who did not appear to interfere with the running of the club. Then in the early 80s we lost the clubhouse to the building of the M25 and lost the 1st and 18th holes. Many of us thought the shareholders, notable Roy, brother Bill Betts, Mick Latham, would pocket the money and run. They didn't and financed the building of a new clubhouse, not to everyone's liking, and built two new holes preserving a good length of over 6000 yards. In hindsight, not a bad job but we humans don't take easy to change.

Then many more members were let in including in one go 50 disillusioned golfers from the Drift Golf Club. It became like a pay and play club, so crowded that the last two competitions I entered I was allotted start times of 6.45 and 11.45. The final straw was in September 1985 when I turned up one Saturday afternoon for a few holes to find a group of 30 Japanese on the first tee waiting to play. That was enough.

Q. So what did you do?

A. I was anxious to maintain my 12 handicap so contacted the English Golf Union for their advice. Tough luck, if you were not a member of a club affiliated to them, there was no way you could maintain a handicap. How outrageous. It got me thinking of the "us and them" syndrome and the "I'm all right Jack, pull up the drawbridge" mentality. Not long after this I launched The Golf Club of Great Britain but that is a story on its own.

I applied to join three clubs, Burhill from whom I never got a reply, Surbiton where I went for an interview, they lost the note so a second interview followed then the "don't call us, we'll call you" reply and the

Bernard Pendry

RAC. Coincidently the day I received the rebuff from Surbiton I received an invite to join the RAC. In hindsight it was more fortunate than I thought at the time. (In later years, post retirement, I grew a pony tail, much to the dismay of some RAC members one of whom commented "if you had had that pony tail at your interview you would never have got in" I took great delight replying "with my credentials I wasn't asked to a interview". Such are some of the members.

Q. Do you have a favourite golfer?

A. Lee Trevino, without hesitation.

Q. Why?

A. He was a one off, not only a great golfer and winner of 6 majors but so enjoyed the game, smiling and chatting even in the tightest of situations. His quips are legendary for instance (a) when it is thundering and lightning hold up a one iron, because even God can't hit a one iron (I think God got his own back because Lee was struck by lightning twice) (b) when an opponent said "I don't like talking during a round". Lee replied "that's OK I'll talk for both of us" (c) the easiest shot in golf is the fourth putt and (d) you hear the highly paid pros complaining about pressure. "I'll tell you what pressure is, it is playing for $20 when you only have $5 in your pocket which was the case many times in my caddying days and taught me there was no option but to win".

The other golfer I loved reading about was Walter Hagen. What style the man had who single handedly revolutionized the way golf professionals were viewed by the golfing establishment in England. Golf pros were considered in the same light as traders and were not permitted into the clubhouse. At the 1920 Open at Deal, Hagan was refused permission to enter the clubhouse so he had his chauffer drive his Rolls Royce to the front of the clubhouse, set up a table and chair and preceded to drink champagne poured by his chauffeur/butler. He also used it as his changing room. Not long after the establishment's whole attitude changed and pros were welcomed as accomplished sportsmen. It took many more years before women were granted the same status.

Q. Were you ever a club thrower?

A. To my utter shame, Yes. I learnt there was a technique to throwing a club so as not to cause damage. Throw it flat so it comes down like a rota blade landing softly in the grass. All very well until one day on the 16th at Leatherhead my 4 wood decided to hit the ball out of bounds. The offending club was hurled scythe fashion and would have landed unharmed had it not been for the seniors tee marker, which was a blue concrete pyramids. My 4 wood hit mid shaft which bent in two. This taught me a salutary lesson and throwing became a rarity.

Q. What are the major changes you have seen over all these years?

A. I suppose the biggest change from when I started is that now everyone has a matched set plus possibly a rescue club. Back when I started you collected the odd club here and there, second hand shops, friends or jumble sales and tried to get a few clubs together. Hickory shafts had been most popular then metal shafts appeared some coated in a covering trying to look like wood and my eight clubs were made up of an assortment of these. There were lovely names, a machie, about a 5 iron, a mashie niblick possibly an eight iron, a brassie now a 3 wood and so on. My 5 iron was heavy and you swung it like a mallet whereas my 4 iron was light and needed a different swing. It was with this motley bag of clubs that I had many enjoyable years, some of the most fun rounds being with Ginge, Archie & Doug none of who progressed to take up the game seriously. The other major change is the composition of the ball, out had gone the original feathery, in came the gutta percha then a ball made up of masses of elastic string wound round a core and coated. Now-a-days there are so many makes of ball none of which makes any difference to my game. The making of a "feathery" is interesting and I like to ask the question "what has a top hat and a spiked breast plate got in common?" The answer is a top hat was filled with feathers, the maker adorned a breast plate with a spike in the middle then had to force the

Bernard Pendry

whole hat full of feathers into a leather pouch and then sew up the pouch and beat it until it could pass as round. Can you imagine what such a procedure would cost today?

Q. If you had your time over again, what changes would you make?

A. David and Eddie thank you for your interest but I am questioned out. Maybe another time I'll let you know about the Golf Club of Great Britain and the good times I am still having at the RAC. For now, fetch me another beer.

APPENDIX 2

HUMOROUS ANECDOTES

THE WORLD OF CLASSICAL MUSIC

When I bought the Mercedes 280SE from Brian Palmer, a client, it had a quadraphonic music system and he had left some 8 tracks of classical music. I had never been interested in classical music but some sounded very pleasant so I said to my kids I might buy a record or two.

I forgot all about this so was surprised when the kids bought me a 33 record of the classics as my Christmas present. Pleased, I went into the lounge, put it on the record player and sat back in my armchair and was thoroughly enthralled listening to this new found music. The kids came in "Dad" me "Don't disturb me I'm enjoying your present." "Dad", me "What do you want?" "You're playing it on the wrong speed". So endeth my appreciation of the classics.

PUTTING MY FOOT IN IT

It was quite a ritual on a Friday night after playing squash and 3 card brag for a few of us to wander over to the local Indian Restaurant, commonly known as 'Argys'. On this particular night Roy Oldaker, a regular, brought along his friend Ray Trafford a known hard man who could sort out anyone. During the evening the name of a local gypsy type family came up, The Hardwicks. I said "I met them once and don't they have two ugly daughters" to which Ray replied, "I'm married to one". Back peddling fast I said, "Well one of them is quite nice". Luckily he saw the funny side and we all had a good laugh.

Bernard Pendry

SQUASH TRIP TO PARIS

A few of us went for a long weekend in Paris. At Gatwick Airport Charlie Tunbridge asked Hank, the Ozzie, to mind his bag while he goes to the loo. Hank promptly puts the bag down rather heavily on the tiled floor and there is whisky all over the place, the bottle having broke. In Paris we were dining at an unusual restaurant up in an attic on a long table with views out of a small window framing the Eiffel Tower. Main meal over, they served strawberries and cream. Brian Sargent sitting on my right had one large strawberry left, no doubt saving the best to last. Being on his left I pointed out the widow and said "Look Brian what a wonderful view of the Eifel Tower". Turning back his strawberry had disappeared. He was not amused.

SAMMY DAVIS AND LIONEL BLAIR

23rd May 1960, Sheila and our first wedding anniversary. I had booked to see Complacent Lover at the Strand Theatre, thoroughly enjoyable so Sheila thought that was the end of the treat but walking back to Piccadilly Circus I lead her into The Pigalle Night Club where Sammy Davis was to perform. As it was a late booking our table was farthest from the stage just outside the door where the waiters were in and out. Before the dinner was served the manager asked if we would like a table nearer the stage. Sheila hesitated but I immediately said "yes" so he led us to a table in the second row just behind Lionel Blair's table.

Well when Sammy came out Lionel went into ecstasy and jumping and with arms waving in the air he danced about shouting "Oh Sammy you're so wonderful, I love you" and went on for about a minute. I imagine the audience had the same opinion as me "what a plonker".

THE TURKEY THAT DIDN'T GET EATEN

Christmas 1970 and it was just dinner for Sheila, the kids and I. Sheila had prepared everything, turkey from Iceland, Brussels sprouts, roast potatoes, parsnips you name it.

The frozen turkey had been taken out of the freezer on 23rd and put in the garage to thaw. About 10 a.m. Mark was asked to bring it in. He appeared holding the tray at arms length, on which the turkey rested, saying, "Are we really going to eat this?" It stank, Sheila burst into tears, I led the boys and together with the turkey we set off to the end of the garden, still in our dressing gowns, dug a hole and there is a photo of me dropping the turkey in. The boys took delight in burying it.

Back at the house Sheila was distraught, "what do we do now" she wailed. "Don't panic I'll find somewhere". The first 4 places I phoned were full but what is now The Boogie Lounge in Epsom had room so all was saved and we had a happy Christmas lunch.

I took the matter up with Iceland who admitted they had had other complaints but when I asked them to refund the extra costs I had incurred all they would do was refund the price of the turkey.

THE SOUP SPILL – RAC 1989

Having just been accepted as a member of The Royal Automobile Club I asked Pam if she would like to have Sunday lunch at my new club. Of course. So arriving about 12.30 I just asked to book a table for two to be informed that it was fully booked. Not being defeated I discussed the situation with the maître d giving him a sob story of how this was my and my wife's first visit and the trouble we had getting there. He was understanding and said "a resident who booked a table has so far not appeared and that if they have not arrived by 2 o'clock you can have their table". After a drink in the bar a waiter came and announced we could have lunch. Walking into the restaurant a pianist was playing soothing tunes as we were shown to our table, right in the middle of the room. We agreed it was a wonderful place and how lucky we were to be here. It was a set menu and up came the starter, minestrone soup. Picking up the conical shaped saltcellar it slipped through my fingers, hit the back of the plate and we sat in horror watching the soup spread over the tablecloth like an advancing army. Pam froze; I tried spooning it back into the plate with little success and was so relieved when a waiter appeared to remedy the situation.

Bernard Pendry

RAY SAUNDERS AND THE STAIRCASE

It was a Christmas Day drink at The Prince Albert Pub at the bottom of Kingston Hill, all the family were there plus Ray and Eileen all nicely seated in the lounge. I had a wander looking for the loo and came across a secluded staircase at the rear. It had handrails on both sides and I wondered if anyone could go down just using the handrails (these thoughts are typical of the way my mind works). Anyway I got the men to have a go. First up was Mike who with a bit of an effort made it down without his feet touching the floor. Next Dave had a go and managed it. Ray, being a very competitive type, had to have a go just to show the youngsters he was still up for it. Well he struggled going from one side to the other, got to within four steps from the bottom when his arms gave way and he headed down his face coming to a sliding halt across the coconut mat at the bottom like Concorde landing. We didn't know whether to laugh or be concerned. This was decided when he got up, his face bright red. Luckily it was only superficial. He was on his way to meet daughter Clare from Gatwick Airport. What a surprise she had wanting to know all about his accident!

FAMILY IN L.A. CINEMA

Sometimes the visit to the cinema is not enjoyable like when staying at cousin Bill's in LA, Mark aged 16 took Michael 12 and sister Nicola 9 to the local cinema. Even in those days they had multiviewing and Mark booked for *Rust Never Sleeps* a Neil Young musical. It didn't take long for his siblings to know they didn't like the film so they walked out intending to go to one of the other cinemas. It was a bit of a maze wandering around but they found another door and in they went to find it was the same place. So endured the rest of the film. I don't think they ever forgave Mark.

FUNNIES AT THE POKER TABLE

Many years ago Dennis, Sheila's second husband, joined our regular school saying he was not sure of the rules for Texas Holdem, a fairly new concept but knew the basics. During the playing of a hand, with the flop on the table, he stood up clutching his back and wondered round the room appearing to be in agony. When the hand was finished with him winning we asked what was the matter, "It was nothing to do with my back I just had to have a look at the board (Mark had hung a board on the wall behind Dennis's chair setting out the priority of the various hands) and I wanted to see if my flush beat a run".

It became a regular feature of our Thursday night games to break at about 9 o'clock for sausages, brought by Graham "Porky" White, a variety of cheeses and a glass or two of red wine making for some amusing conversation. Son Mark in those days was known to be a gannet with a passion for the cheese. While he and Alan Borley were finishing a hand, son Mike went into the kitchen got what looked like a cheese but actually was a winter seeded lard block for the birds, cut it into pieces knowing that Mark would have a bite. However Alan returned first and before we could stop him, took a big bite. It was only a second or two before he spat it out but the deed was done prompting jibes such as "Do you fly away in the winter?" "Do you want a mirror or a bell to play with?" and on it went.

Mike bought along American Mike who he was employing, and he fitted in well. Chatting as one does in the break he recounted the story of how he got into poker in nam. We were impressed. "You actually went to Vietnam?" "No, I said my Nan taught me."

THE HEAD. 1943

Dad's friend, Bernard Williams, was an undertaker in Fulham and in 1943 was asked to collect the body of a local who had died in a dance hall in Tooting about five miles away when it was hit with a bomb. He travelled there in his hearse but on arrival he was informed that the head of the body could not be found so it was only the headless body that had a ride in the hearse. A few days later he was informed that the head had been found. No way was he going to waste precious petrol to take the hearse so took the 630 trolley bus. He came back with the head in a hatbox! Yuck!

Bernard Pendry

SINGING IN MONTE CARLO

I had been beside Nick Preece at all the meetings leading up to successfully selling Redmans, his estate agency business, so as an extra special thanks he invited Pam & I to join him and wife Sally for a long weekend at The Monte Carlo Beach Hotel. Such a grand place if you don't worry about the prices, I didn't worry as it was his treat and the menus given us were "Ladies menus" i.e. with no prices displayed. We had dined in the Hermitage Hotel, taking our coffee and wine to the lounge where a smart pianist was tinkling on the ivories. We started dancing, there was only one other guest, an elderly lady who told us she lived in Paris but liked to winter at The Hermitage, who complemented Pam and me on our jiving. The pianist asked if we had any requests, knowing Nick's favourite was Fats Domino singing "On Blueberry Hill" so I started singing "I lost my thrill on Blueberry Hill" when he stopped me, saying, "I've got it" and merrily started playing *"Down Mexico Way"*. So ended any thought of a singing career.

AN UNEXPECTED SWIM

In my young cycling days one of our favorite rides was to Runnymede to enjoy being besides the river Thames. This is as reported by Alex Drury "on this sunny day we had padlocked our bikes to walk along the riverside path, saddlebags under our arms when someone called, I heard a splash, and turning around expecting to see Bernard but all I saw was his saddlebag and cap floating on the water soon followed by him coming up for air spluttering. Apparently he had turned to see who was calling and promptly walked right into the river.

WHO WAS AT THE DOOR?

Nicely settled on a Sunday after lunch with Dad in the best armchair, there was knock on the front door, I said it couldn't be for me so Dad went to find there was nobody there so returning to the back room who is lounging in his chair? Reg of course.

MY TEXAN FRIEND.

Curtis, a Texan friend I met in Rome, was staying with us and having a general chat with the family he was asked what his hobbies were. "Well I enjoy a game of golf with my buddies but what we like best of all is going out into the forests shooting coons". Everyone gasps and said "Surely not". Seeing the horror on our faces he replied "Not coons, raccoons." Curtis and wife Glender stayed with us a couple of times, lovely people but we were mildly horrified when first she wandered around the kitchen dental flossing her teeth and Curtis with his feet on the table cutting his toe nails. I think Americans are somewhat different.

MUM AND HER KNOCKERS

Mum was in the lovely Milverton Care Home in Long Ditton, Surrey, and brother Reg & I would visit her most Fridays for a singsong.

On one of these occasions a well-endowed, charming black nurse was leaning over Mum adjusting her pillow, Mum, pointing at her bosom, said, "I used to have a pair like that". We couldn't stop giggling.

Bernard Pendry

APPENDIX 3

THE JOY OF CINEMAS

After the war cinemas were soon booming and I enjoyed my fair share. Mondays I would go with Mum on a 14 bus on the Fulham Road either south to Putney or north to Walham Green (changed to Fulham Broadway on 16th February 1952). My earliest memories are Dumbo, which made me cry when his mummy was taken away, then Bambi who's Dad got shot in the first few minutes.

Pure magic was Saturday Morning Pictures specifically for kids. The organ would come up out of a pit playing any tune that we could all sing along to. Regulars were Abbott & Costello, Roy Rogers with Dale Evans and horse Trigger; nobody ever got shot, Jonny Weissmuller as Tarzan, The Bowery Boys with Mugs McGuiness and best of all, Flash Gordon v Emperor Ming, the forerunner of Star Wars. There was this 'toy' space ship going round in a circle and you could see the cord that was pulling it round. All very magical. If it was a cowboy film it didn't matter which one, you couldn't hear a thing because if they wore a white hat they were goodies and you cheered, if a black hat they were baddies you booed with such gusto it completely drowned out the sound of the film. The guy who came up playing the organ always got a cheer, he always asked if any birthdays, which there always was and we had another loud sing along. Later it was the Bob Hope & Bing Crosby 'Road To' films that were as funny as Abbott & Costello but we didn't find Laurel & Hardy to our tastes. Isn't it funny that whereas the first to now seem dated Laurel & Hardy have survived the test of time.

Later with schoolmates we went all over the place going to the 'flicks' two or three times a week. Out of interest appendix 3a is a list of the films during these years. Some of the films from those days that still live vividly in my memory are 'They Died' with Their Boots On', Errol Flynn as

Colonel Custer being annihilated at the battle on 'the Little Big Horn' by Chief Sitting Bull and Chief Crazy Horse, 'The Wizard of Oz' with Judy Garland which I found very scary, 'Mighty Joe Young', a "King Kong" look alike and many more.

In those long gone days, the programmes started with a B movie, usually a sub standard film by an up and coming producer, followed by the Pathe News and then the main film. Costs in 1953 were 1/3d front rows and 1/6p further back or the balcony. (Shillings and pence equivalent to 6p and 7.5 p in today's money).

If a film were for over 16s I'd wear brother Reg's jacket that was so big it hung down over my shoulders but nobody queried. Did I ever bunk in? Someone told me that with a piece of looped wire you could insert it into a side door, it would then wrap around the exit bar, a pull and in you went. I think I was too scared of being caught to try it.

On 6th February 1952 it was announced that all cinemas would be closed in respect of the King's funeral

My favourite film of all times is *Genevieve* about the RAC veteran car rally from Hyde Park Corner to Brighton. It featured Kay Kendal and her huge St. Bernard dog travelling with Kenneth Moore racing against Dinah Sheridan and John Gregson both in old cars pre 1905. Some incredibly funny scenes. Other films that have a memorable effect are *'Towering Inferno'* where I came out with sweaty palms, and *'Jaws'*: I wouldn't go in the bath for ages. Another film that had me roaring with laughter and heard by my sister-in-law who said to her then fiancé "my brother-in-law is in the balcony" to which he asked how she knew, reply being "I can hear him laughing" it was Danny Kaye in **Merry Andrew.**

All so different to today's multiscreens, Netfix and Everyman cinemas were you sit in lounger type seats and have food and drinks served to you and 3D where monsters can jump out at you.

What would we do without films? Sue & I regularly go to Epsom Odeon.

I wonder what the future is going to bring?

Bernard Pendry

APPENDIX TO APPENDIX 3

A SELECTION OF FILMS SEEN IN 1952/53

THEY DIED WITH THEIR BOOTS ON

ERROL FLYN IN CUSTERS LAST STAND.

DUMBO

THE FIRST FILM THAT MADE ME CRY

WIZARD OF OZ

JUDY GARLAND. MESMERISING

GONE WITH THE WIND

WENT ON TOO LONG FOR A TEENAGER.

GOOD MORNING BOYS

WILL HAY THE HEADMASTER

PALEFACE

BOB HOPE IN THE WILD WEST

SCOTT OF THE ANTARTIC

SUCH A SAD ENDING

THE SECRET LIFE OF WALTER MITTIE

DANNY KAYE. SUCH A LAUGH

WHISKEY GALORE

FUN IN SCOTLAND, FREE WHISKEY

WHITE HEAT

JAMES CAGNEY

MEET THE KILLER

ABBOTT & COSTELLO. ALWAYS FUN

EAST OF THE RISING SUN

SPENCER TRACY & JAMES STEWART

THE BIG STEEL

ROBERT MITCHAM

THE BLUE LAMP

JACK WARNER P.C. 49

12 O'CLOCK HIGH

GREGORY PECK

MORNING DEPARTURE

SIR JOHN MILLS. SUBMARINE LOST

GAS BAGS

THE CRAZY GANG

TREASURE ISLAND

ADVENTURE FOR KIDS

ROGUES OF SHERWOOD FOREST

ROBIN HOOD AND ALL THAT

THE JOLSON STORY

AL JOLSON. BEST SINGER EVER

WHERE NO VULTURES FLY

DINAH SHERIDAN. AFRICA

RETURN OF THE APE MAN

BELA LUGOSI. ALWAYS SCARY.

TARZAN AND THE GREEN GODESS

BRUCE BENNETT

TREASURE OF THE LOST CANYON

WILLIAM POWELL

MURDER INC.

HUMPHREY BOGART

MIGHTY JOE YOUNG

NOT QUITE AS GOOD AS KING KONG

FLAME OF THE BARBARY COAST

JOHN WAYNE

SAILORS BEWARE

DEAN MARTIN & JERRY LEWIS

AFRICAN QUEEN

HUMPHREY BOGART & KATHRINE HEPBURN

HOLD THAT BABY

THE BOWERY BOYS

ROAD TO BALI

BING CROSBY & BOB HOPE

SNOWS OF KILIMANJARO

GREGORY PECK & AVA GARDNER

THE CRIMSON PIRATE

BURT LANCASTER & NICK CRAVAT

SPRINGFIELD RIFLE

GARY COOPER & PHYLIS THAXTER

THE BAD AND THE BEAUTIFUL

BURT LANCASTER

TWICE UPON A TIME

BEST FILM EVER (FORGET WHY)

SHANE

ALAN LADD

VEILS OF BAGDAD

VICTOR MATURE

FAVORITES

ANY TARZAN FILM WITH JOHNNY WEISSMULLER

THE ROAD FILMS WITH CROSBY & HOPE

ANY WESTERN

ALL ABBOTT & COSTELLO

LATER ON THE FUNNIEST FILM EVER

GENEVIEVE. THE VETERAN CAR RUN TO BRIGHTON

Bernard Pendry

APPENDIX 4

CARS

THE 1928 AUSTIN 7 (No I didn't buy it new)

The year was 1954; I was 18 and looking for my first car. Babe (Alan Dodsworth, called Babe because he was the youngest by far of 4 brothers) had this 1928 Austin 7 for some time and agreed to sell it to me for the princely sum of £12.10.0. It was British racing green and with a fair wind could get up to 45 M.P.H.; it was Sheila and my pride and joy.

At the time I was living at home, Ringmer Avenue and saw Archie (Norris Argyrou) on a fairly regular basis even though he lived over in Highbury. If any of my schoolmates were technical it had to be Archie but I say this with tongue in cheek. He was the one who when we took a motorboat out from Looe in Cornwall took along a spanner and screwdriver so he could make the boat go fasted. We rowed back in! Anyway, when the Austin started loosing too much oil we decided to take out the engine and completely rebuild it down in the basement. Many trips were made to the one shop that stocked parts for these old vehicles and it was over in Clapham High Road. Big ends, small ends, gaskets and lots of other bits whose names now escape me. I remember the worst problem was getting out bolts from the engine block and in the end I think there was still one left out.

The day finally came when we had done everything we knew how to, (the carburetor remained a mystery), and together we lifted it out of the basement and lowered it into place. All the connections made, it was time for the big test, would it start? Mum was out watching proceedings; I was in the car while Archie cranked the starting handle. Once, twice and then bingo, it went like a dream. Mum let out a cry "Hallelujah".

The Austin had an all alloy body so there was no rust but other things definitely needed attention not least of which was the leaking radiator, at one stage I drove around with a large watering can in the back. People gave all sorts of advice, mustard, Holt's rad seal but the beauty was "an egg". Having unsuccessfully tried the other two the egg had to be tried, so gingerly I put an egg in my pocket (no it didn't break), Sheila and I drove up the road because the engine had to be hot before the egg was broken into the radiator. I unscrewed the radiator cap, cracked the egg on the side and like Phillip Harben (top chef in those days), let the egg tenderly disappear into the radiator and off we went. It did the trick for some considerable time but when I looked into the radiator the yoke was sitting on the fins hard-boiled where it remained.

I had been driving the Austin for over a year when I decided to put in for my driving test. The test center was in Wimbledon, South West, London. I felt reasonably confident, knew all about the dangerous cross roads on the route but there could be a problem with the emergency stop. Archie and I had renewed the brake pads but they were operated by cables, which stretch, and although there were three shortening calipers on each side you could hardly call them efficient. My first shock was when the examiner informed me that another colleague, an inspector, would be coming along. I informed him that the car was very small but he said as long as it was not a two seater it would be all right. Somehow the extra got into the back and had to prostrate himself every time I wanted to look out of the rear window. All went well and then we came to the emergency stop. He slapped his folder on the dashboard, I rammed my foot on the foot brake, yanked on the hand brake and the Austin coasted to a graceful stop. I passed.

I had the car for some years, during the courting days with Sheila and into the marriage years when we lived at Gwalia Road in Putney. One Sunday morning, a boyhood friend, Brian Davis from Ringmer Avenue who was now living just up the road, came knocking at the door in an agitated state to announce that my beloved Austin was lying on its side, evidently turned over by Saturday night revelers leaving St. Mary's Dance Hall. No problem. We just turned it back onto its 4 wheels.

I didn't push my luck by going on any long journeys with the one exception. Archie had a 1934 most intriguing shaped Austin 7 the likes of which I have not seen before or since, it was open top with a bee like rear end. He was at a loose end so we agreed to go somewhere like the New Forest for the weekend. Sheila came with me and sister Eileen went with Archie (it must have been the time before she met Ray). We fairly flew along keeping to a steady 45 and at times bordering 50 down hill. Oh! What heady and happy days.

The beginning of the end came when driving home from a dance at the Chelsea Town Hall with Eileen and Ray the half shaft went so we had to push it home. I replaced it with a second hand one, which really was not a proper fit and made a grinding noise so it wasn't driven much thereafter. We were offered £10.00 for its alloy scrap value. What a sad end.

THE MORRIS MINOR 850

With Sheila we moved up market to a Morris Minor only 850cc not the 'fast' 1000 (cost £285 with 31,500 miles on the clock). Quite down market compared with the other cars driven by the gang I played squash with at Wimbledon Squash & Badminton Club. Last car without power steering. I hadn't realized the difference it makes.

Next cars were Dagenham dustbins, e.g. Fords. A pale blue **Cortina 1300** really smart PAN 103E, a low profile white **Cortina 1600** bought from client Brian Palmer. This was something of a collectors car and performed really well.

THE MERCEDES

Thought I would go one better and bought a **Rover 2500** expecting a good racy car. What a disappointment, sluggish and ideal for an old gent that I wasn't then. It didn't last long so when Brian Palmer wanted to get rid of his **Mercedes 280SE** I jumped in. Possibly the best car I have ever owned. It had quadraphonic sound that could be played at full volume with no distortion and on a Moonfleet Manor trip to play Frazer Court; Dave Timps insisted I play Frampton Comes Alive at full volume. (Must write about the matches against Frazer Court sometime).

I kept this Merc for some years but when it got to 70,000 miles on the clock I thought it time to sell, (stupid me) sold it to Alan Luthwood, a fellow member at Leatherhead Golf Club. He had it for many more years. A bad decision on my part.

THE FORD XR4i AND THE HORSE

I don't know whether this should be under Embarrassing Moments or here in CARS but here goes. Back to Fords and the first car I bought new, a **Ford XR4i**. Did this shift! I got talked into having it *Zibarted* as life long rust preventer. What a nasty smell we had to endure. I took the kids down to the Miles's farm and on the way back was whizzing along a country road when up ahead there were two horse riders plodding along. I didn't think I needed to slow down too much but as I went past the lead horse shied out and took the whole rear bumper off my new car. Well it was like being in front of a firing squad as people seemed to appear from everywhere and accused me of reckless driving and even the kids were on their side. Didn't matter to them that the horse seemed unperturbed. Had to tie the bumper up and limp off in disgrace.

SPEEDING

I had been done for speeding in the XR4i when leaving Effingham Golf Course going towards Leatherhead. So next time I left this club I went cross-country north to the main A3. I was in no particular hurry but suddenly realized I was doing 110 m.p.h. Just then I spotted in the rear view mirror a car some way back flashing their headlights. Immediately I reduce speed to 70 (the speed limit) and watched as this car got closer. It was not a police car so I was a bit cautious in case it was trouble. The car overtook me and waived me into the side. Gingerly I pulled over but ready to hare off if it was anything suspicious. Out got two uniformed police and two plane-clothed police. The conversation went like this PC "do you know you have been speeding?" me "I thought you had to tail me some distance before you knew my speed" PC "Put it like this, we were tailing a car doing 85 m.p.h. and ready to stop him when you went past like a rocket. However we are only going to book you for 89 m.p.h. so you won't lose your license" me "fair cop and thanks".

FASTEST CAR THE FORD COSWORTH

Wanting something special I bought a Ford Cosworth 0 to 60 in 5.9 seconds. . The problem was that you felt like racing all the time strapped in the bucket seats as the engine purred. One morning entering the A3 at the Robin Hood round-a-bout a Ford Escort X was on my tail so I thought I would burn him off but reaching 120 mph I chickened out. It didn't last long as I took Alan Pratt to a bridge club in Twickenham and coming out the car was gone, the only thing left was the door lock on the ground. The police said there was little hope of recovery because this car would have been stolen to order and was now either abroad or being stripped down for racing. The insurance company were good, I got back most of the £17,000.

BMW

I bought a black **BMW320**. Thinking this would be a bit racy. It was smart and comfortable, a cut above the average but nothing special.

NOW TO JAGUARS

 My first **Jaguar** was a car to be proud of, a Guy Salmon showroom model costing £19,000. The most exciting ride was when Pam & I went to Norfolk for a RAC rally with 20 other cars. We were first coming out of a west Norfolk stately home heading for an east Norfolk toy railway station when we were overtaken by a TVR who sped away. Well I had never tried the 'S' button before but it worked and I raced after the TVR across country going round bends and flat out on the straights like I had never done before. We drove into the railway car park together and the driver complemented me on being able to stay with him. This was a once in a lifetime experience. This Jag lasted 10 years and I was so pleased with Jaguars that with Sue traded it in for a new XE Prestige model £33,000 in December 2015.

CARS AND MY WIVES

Cars were not always kind to my wives. In the 70s I bought Sheila a Mini Cooper S, fast little thing that she enjoyed driving. I made a big mistake by telling her that it cornered like on rails. Well one evening she took off with Pam heading for Cobham. Approaching the A3 at Tolworth she put the cornering to the test, hit the far wall, which bounced her back to mount the low wall of the Toby Jug Pub. Both were in shock and she was surprised when it wouldn't go in reverse. Hence the RAC had to be called.

I was lunching with Nick Preece in Liberty Bells Restaurant in Surbiton when having just finished the starter and started on a bottle of wine his mobile rang (I had not yet aspired to such modern devices). It was a neighbour "Pam's OK but". Without hesitation we were on our way and the restaurateur just said go. Kind man, as we may not have returned to pay the bill. The scene we found was like out of a war zone, walls were down, her new Honda Civic car was in a sorry state, two tyres flat and at peculiar angles, and the rear back side caved in.

We found Pam in bed tended by Joan a neighbour. We asked what had happened and she told us the story "I was sweeping up the leaves in the front garden and there were a few under the car so I thought I would just sit in sideways put it into reverse to move it a foot or so, well it shot backwards at high speed, I must have put my foot on the accelerator instead of the brake all I heard was smashing and crashing totally out of control. It finally came to a halt. Shakily I got out to find the car on a pile of bricks on the pavement. A lorry driver pulled up "Are you OK" and when I said "no" he drove off.

We asked how she felt now. She replied, "Shaky but otherwise OK" to which Nick commented, "well you now know your vocation in life, a demolition expert". We got her out of bed then went back and finished our lunch and wine.

The only thing my third wife, Sue, did was to stop at a red light but got a penalty notice because the front tyres were over the stop line. Complain as I did they would not squash the notice. I took the rap and spent the most boring 3 hours in a re-training programme.

THE CLAMP AND POLICE

I don't know whether it should be here but my car was the cause. It was in 2003 we had friends Glenda & Curtis from Texas staying with us and we treated them to see Les Miserable. I drove to Surbiton Station where I parked at 6 p.m. and off to town we went. Lovely show followed by a light Chinese meal and a beer and then home.

Back in the car park an attendant was wondering around and when I asked what he was doing he said "your clamped." I protested that it was now 10 p.m. but was informed it was 24 hours parking so I owed £50.00. I said there was no chance of paying such an outrageous fine and told Pam and our guests to get in the car. The attendant was yelling that he would call the police, which scared the Americans, but I insisted so in they got.

When I started to drive there was a scraping noise that didn't seem to cause a problem so I drove slowly up the side road and onto the main road closely followed by the attendant. A few yards further I thought 'this is silly' so stopped and went back to the attendant and offered to pay the £50.00. "Not possible", came the reply "I have already called the police." So on I crawled. About a quarter of a mile further I saw a police car with lights flashing approaching from the other direction so I stopped and turned off the lights. It turned left into a side road quickly to reappear and drove right in front of me at the same time as another police car pulled in behind me plus an unmarked car stopped opposite and two plain clothed guys rushed over instructing me to get out of the car, face the car, spread my legs and frisked me. At the same time two senior police officers appeared and asked if I had been drinking "just one pint officer" as the resulting Breathalyzer proved. Having great faith in our police force I was not in the least worried but our American friends were shitting themselves and told Pam to stay put when she wanted to get out.

It now got very convivial but they said I had to be arrested, on what charge I asked "damaging third parties property." The CLAMP was a heavy pyramid shape piece of metal with a chain that had been looped over the steering column.

Now the car had to be moved, one of the policemen got in, put it into reverse and promptly backed into the rear police car but no damage. Luckily there was a taxi office just over the road so Pam hired a cab and took our friends home while the two plain clothed police took me in their car to Kingston Police Station. On the way they said that from the call out they thought there was a raving drunk driving the car, it also turned out we were all members of Mid Surrey Squash Club.

At the police station it was all very pleasant but after finger printing me they said I would have to go into a cell basically for my own safety, while they discussed the case with the Duty sergeant. Having never been in a police cell before it was quite daunting, bare walls, concrete toilet, concrete bed so what I did was my norm, lay down and went to sleep. It wasn't long before I was let out and told I was free to go. "What about my car?" to which the reply was "nothing to do with us, it is up to you and the clamping company" so at midnight I was out searching for a taxi. All this time Pam was having to assure our guests that everything would be all right.

In the morning Curtis and I hired bolt cutters and went round to rescue the car, throwing the clamp in the boot. So the clamping company not only did not get their £50.00 but also lost a clamp.

And now for something different, a **MOTOR BIKE.**

After years of commuting by public transport, Southern train then underground, to central London daily was a drag, wasted 2 hours plus each day. Right out side the office was a motorbike park, which got me thinking so I contacted mate, Babe Dodsworth to ask his advice. (Babe had always been into motorbikes and owned about 8). I told him I wanted one for travelling to town and thought a 125 h.p. would suffice.

Bernard Pendry

"No way, you need a work horse" came the advice and soon he helped me buy a Honda 400/4.

I used this every weekday and it was so liberating and thrilling knowing whatever the traffic you would get home in good time. However it did have its downside. Coming home one February evening approaching the Kingston-by-pass (this was before it became a dual carriage way) there was only one car in the road but straddling both lanes so I flashed, it started to pull over but when I pulled out to over take it pulled back so I accelerated doing about 60 m.p.h. when all of a sudden I was flying through the air bouncing along the road watching the bike on its side sliding along side. The car didn't stop and when I finished bouncing I thought I should be hurt but nothing seemed to be wrong. Someone must have phoned for an ambulance as one appeared and whisked me to Kingston Hospital. Nothing was found to be wrong so home I went. The kids wanted to know what had happened so by car we visited the scene. Apparently what had happened was that a lorry had demolished the light on a central curb and I had run straight into it. Result was I had a claim against the council because the temporary light they had erected had fallen over. I did threaten to sue the council but accepted their offer of £500.

The end of my bike riding was one icy winter's morning I slithered and slipped as far as Tolworth, said to myself "you must be mad" turned around and went home.

However if I ever had to regularly commute to town I would get another motorbike.

APPENDIX 5

CYCLING

I remember the first time I attempted a two-wheel bike, I think it must have been one borrowed. On I got with Dad holding the saddle and off I set, great no problem but how do I stop? There I was careering down Ringmer Avenue fast approaching the T-junction with Munster Road yelling, "help" when some kind man ran out and held me. Soon I learnt what brakes were for.

Soon about age 12 I bought a junior racing bike from mate Deesie, racing gears, drop handlebars. Had it for a few years and so enjoyed going on trips to Wimbledon Common and Richmond Park.

I had basically out grown it so Dad was going to buy me one as a 1948 Christmas present, would it be a racer, drop handlebars, 10 speed gears and lightweight? Oh no, it was heavy, upright, Sturmie Archer gears and altogether no street cred whatsoever more like a tradesman's bike without the front basket. I tried to smile but it was through gritted teeth and the bike was soon got rid of, the biggest disappointment ever.

Then I bought a proper racing bike and Alex Drury, who had recently returned to his previously bombed house, and I became enthusiastic cyclists sometimes joined by Babe Dodsworth. A favourite run was to Runnymede about 20 miles away that we did many evenings or for days by the river Thames.

Did I ever fall off? Yes, it was on one of Alex's and my evening runs to Runnymede. We were flying along heads down like pursuit racers taking it in turns to lead. Alex was leading with me really close behind when for some reason he momentarily stopped pedaling, my front wheel overtook his rear wheel stopping me from pulling left and over I went. Apart from a sore elbow no damage to either the bike or me.

In those days lorries didn't go too fast so sometimes we would get right in behind one to get caught in its tail draught just inches from its rear, Heaven help us if they put the brakes on. Even more dangerous was when we would just hang on for a free ride, stupid.

Longest ride in one day was from Fulham to Margate and back, approximately 120 miles. There must have been a reason why but whatever it was escapes me. With Alex we did do Oxford and back in a day. Then when Dad took the Six Bells Pub in Colerne, Wiltshire I cycled there a couple of times down the A4 about 100 miles. On the first ride I stopped in Hungerford for a snack in a local café and was amused to hear Guy Mitchell sing She Wears Red Feathers & a Hoola Hoola Skirt. A really catchy tune that I can still sing to this day.

Towards the end of schooling and for a year or so after I cycled to visit many girl friends, of course Kathleen in Wandsworth, Barbara Goodman in Streatham and farthest to Gilliam White over in Tottenham. (Well worth the ride).

Babe Dodsworth, friend from 4 doors away bought a motorbike so it was goodbye to cycles for many years.

THE STOLEN BIKE

Well not quite. Once we moved to Ruxley Lane I used to walk every weekday to Tolworth Station about a mile. One day I spied a bike discarded on a grass bank near the station. It was there for many weeks so I investigated. It was a rusty old thing, the tyres were almost flat but otherwise it did go so I assumed it had been ditched. Rather than let it rot I took it home, pumped up the tyres, washed it down and used it as my transport to the station. Never bothered to chain it up knowing that no one would take this junk heap. One morning I had to go to Victoria Station instead of Waterloo so I cycled to Stoneleigh Station instead of Tolworth and left the bike propped against a fence. Would you believe it, when I arrive back, it was gone. I felt "bloody cheek" and was so annoyed I reported the theft to the local police. Two hours later a young policemen knocked on the door "excuse me sir but was it you who reported a stolen bike?" "Yes" "do you mind telling me where you got the bike?'" So I told him the story of my find. "That bike was stolen from Stoneleigh Station some time ago and the owner reclaimed it today". Making notes in his little notebook he said "I must warn you sir this is very serious case and maybe taken further". After I stopped laughing I told him not to be so ridiculous and I never heard another word.

THE ELECTRIC BIKES

Now 62 years later I invested in an electric bike, recommended by the lady doctor attending Pam in the hospice. This bought a new lease of life as I could go riding with the kids. Ex daughter-in-law, Jake was a keen cyclist and was breaking all records at her club so I thought I would go riding with her and her club friends assuming with this new power I could ride with them. We set off from Horton Country Park, just half a mile away and they said, "not going too far today, only down to Dorking". They must be joking as that is all of 26 miles but I thought I would go some of the way. Next I didn't realise how fast they ride, by law my maximum is 15 mph was like walking pace to them. I made Ashtead then left them and diverted to the RAC Club.

Now Sue has returned we regularly go cycling. At first she had an ordinary bike but she had difficulty keeping up we me so off to Halfords for a Pendleton electric bike so we go off in every direction within a 20-mile radios, Epsom and Ashtead commons, Richmond Park, Windsor and Bushy Parks, along river towpaths and as far as Wimbledon Common. Further afield we load the bikes onto the Jaguar cycle rack for day trips and always take them on holidays, the best being a week's holiday touring along the south coast visiting various croquet clubs and the local towns.

What could have been a very serious accident happened in 2019 when Alex and his sister Aria, grandchildren of Eileen & Ray Saunders, were staying with us for the weekend. They borrowed bikes from our neighbours and off we set in single file with me leading the way over a regular route through our estate and towards the Horton Nature Reserve. As I tuned left to go on a side path Alex must have thought it would be clever to over take me on the inside. He clipped my front wheel and I went sprawling head first landing full force on my left shoulder. What I yelled at him is not fit for print. It took almost a year for my shoulder to recover but it could have been worse.

VALLEY OF THE KINGS

FAMILY AT DORSET VILLAS

FAIR COP ON WAY TO
THE GRAND CANYON

TRADITIONAL DRESS
AT MILDEN HALL

BBQ AT MILDEN HALL   *EGYPT*

MILDEN HALL   *EGYPT*

WAVE ROCK WESTERN AUSTRALIA

*BLACKPOOL'S
FAMOUS BALLROOM*

JET SKIING AT SUN CITY

PORT DOUGLAS

Bernard Pendry

A TIPPLE WHILE WAITING
FOR THE LADIES

ME ON BIKE

DAVID & ED

PAT SHADBOLT

MY SWING

KATHLEEN

GILLIAN

Bernard Pendry

APPENDIX 6

EMBARRASSING MOMENTS

Being particularly thick skinned I found only a few of the following incidences embarrassing but as you will see others did. Doug Hudson, my old school boy chum, used to say "Bern embarrass me now and get it over with."

****

The earliest that springs to mind is the time that I had a girlfriend round on a Sunday, which one I do not remember, it may have been Sheila but I think it was pre Sheila and on the Monday evening my Dad called me aside and said "Mother had a shock today when she found a French letter in the wash. It must have been Reg as I know it wouldn't be you." I could have kept schtum but honour made me own up.

****

In the early days of courting Sheila I took her to the new milk shake bar in Putney with the trendy name of *Hi Jean*. On the menu was "mushroom soup *with stalks*". I had never heard of such a thing but it was worth a try so I ordered it. Up came the soup and search as I might I couldn't find a trace of a "stalk". This wasn't on, they advertised 'with stalks' and stalks I wanted. A discussion ensued and the waiter said "Sir some you win and some you lose." I did not give up and caused even more of a fuss. Off he went and returned with a plate full of stalks and dumped them in my now tepid soup. The moral of the story must be that Sheila should have realised what kind of boyfriend she had and ran for cover.

****

This one doesn't concern me directly but certainly was embarrassing for the two in question. In our group at school I was reckoned to be the most knowledgeable when it came to the fairer sex so it was me that Stewart turned to when he thought he had a chance of loosing his virginity. In those days it was a trial to pluck up courage to buy a 'packet of three' from a chemist who invariably had a lady assistant. But he had endured this ordeal and now needed some help. He was not sure what to do when the moment came to don the French letter. I explained that timing was important; you had to make certain that the lady (give her the benefit of the doubt) was as committed as you and when he felt the moment was right surreptitiously you unwrap the FL and don it. Then you are away.

Next time I saw Stewart the obvious question was "how did it go?" to which he replied "It was going great, she was as keen as me but I had great difficulty getting the FL on, as you said, I took off the wrapper, **unrolled it** but it was hell's own job to get it on."

****

Those on the wrong end of my antics are definitely my three wonderful children. I am certain that between them they could fill pages of such occasions. Nicola reminded me of the time not long after she had started at the new school, Ewell High. Our house was a regular meeting place as we had the pool table that was a real magnet and along with her stories about our many holidays in far-flung places they thought she came from a very special family. Apparently she had told them all about her Dad and they were suitably impressed and looked forward to meeting me one day. Well that day duly arrived but not in the way Nicola had imagined. I had been off early in the morning for a golf day and back to Lou Rolph's pub, The Red Lion, for lunch and many alcoholic beverages. Naturally I was not driving and was driven home by Nick Preece. As we pulled up opposite the house Nicola and her friends were outside and she announced, "This is my Dad" with pride in her voice. I had not felt too well in the car, staggered out and promptly threw up in the gutter. (Not an impressive debut).

Bernard Pendry

****

I do not make a habit of getting inebriated but golf do's have to take some responsibility. There was this other occasion where we returned to The Red Lion for a feast, prize giving and jollities. Knowing that some of us may be the worse for wear, Keith Hicks offered to take a few of us in his transit van. The only problem was there were no seats in the back so I put a couple of our dining chairs in and off four of us went. Well the do was great but after too much drink I fell asleep on the floor. The doormen wanted to throw me out but Lou explained I was one of the party so they rolled me under a bench seat. When it came time to leave there were only Keith and I in the van and to his frequent question, "which way do we go?" I just kept saying, "Turn left." Well after we passed the pub for the third time he realised he was on his own. When we finally pulled up outside 30 Ruxley I got out with my prize, a big vacuum flask and Keith past out one of the chairs on which I lent. Well the chair began to slide away from me, I tried to correct it but it only went faster and there was me whizzing along leaning on the back of the chair until it out ran me and I went sprawling in the gutter. This commotion brought Michael out of the house and when I stood up with blood pouring down my face he thought I had been set upon and was looking for the culprit ready to do battle. When I finally got up my hard won prize was more like a rattle than a Thermos.

****

Pam had booked middle front row seats for us to see "Evita" (the life story of Eva Peron) at a leading London theatre. The hall became hushed; the lights dimmed and on walked the compare. He stood centre stage in the spot light total silence and we all waited with baited breath. He then said, in a clear voice "One, two, three, four" and paused for a split second when I was heard to say "Five, six, seven, eight." Well the look he gave could have killed and I shrank 6 inches. He then continued, "Welcome Eva Peron." Yes this was truly embarrassing.

****

Another theatre incident. Pam had booked for eight of us to see a show again in a leading West End theatre but when we were shown to our seats by the usherette they were already taken. She explained to the occupants that they were in the wrong seat and after some persuading had them all up and trouping out much to their confusion. At this stage the manager appeared to see what the commotion was all about. Studying both lots of tickets he turned to me and said "Sir, your tickets are for yesterday." Well whom could I blame? I found it quite a laugh; it all ended well when he found us other seats a little further back.

****

2nd March 2003. Wintering at Dona Lola in Macarena C, one of our crowd Naomi, wife of Tommy from SE London, the salt of the earth Cockney, but she has really naff tastes. Over the last two years she has insisted on giving Pam items like golden cherubs, false flowers and the like that you might find in a gypsy caravan. This Sunday morning our Welsh friends, Linda and Geoffrey called round to share a cuppa with us and Eileen and Ray who were staying for a week. In our kitchen waiting to be washed was this OTT glass fruit bowl that had appeared sometime yesterday. I said, "I suppose that fruit bowl is another gift from Naomi". It went quiet then Pam announced that Linda had given it to us. Luckily Linda has a good sense of humour.

• •

Circa early 70s. At a holiday camp with the family they held a fancy dress competition. I was not interested but just before the start I had this "super" idea. There was a cardboard inside of a toilet roll. Somehow I strapped this to my knee, rolled up some red paper and put it on the other end, hung two golf balls underneath and off I went with this edifice covered with a tea towel.

The compare was entertaining quite a few campers with young kids in the front row. When the compare asked what I was, I took away the tea towel and proudly replied a *cockney*. There was this horrendous silence followed by gasps of horror. Possibly inventive but highly inappropriate.

Bernard Pendry

****

Circa 1977. Party at the Squash Club with fancy dress theme. I went having a toilet seat around my neck with bars of Camay soap hanging from it and wearing a pilot's cap. Nobody could guess what I was. Can you? I was a Kamikaze pilot. Get it?

****

Driving to my office in Surbiton with Mark a car pulled right out in front of me. Incensed I whizzed past and pulled up right in front of the car and got out ready to do verbal battle. A quite large gentleman got out, walked up to me and calmly said "I think you should get into your car and drive off." I replied "Good idea" and did as suggested.

Similar incident. Back when I was working for South Bank Estates I was looking out of our 17th floor window down to the junction south of Vauxhall Bridge. There stopped at the lights was a small bubble car when a cyclist drew up along side, got off his bike and was waving a clenched fist at the driver that had obviously cut him up. The door of the small bubble car opened and out got this guy of some 6 feet 6. Now I of course couldn't hear what was said but the cyclist just nodded his head with arms in a surrendering attitude and got back on his bike and rode off.

APPENDIX 7

MY AMOURS

(not for the feint hearted)

Prequel to Amours

These dalliances have mainly occurred when I was single e.g. before I courted Sheila and all went well for 17 years when she became uninterested in love making possibly because she always thought I was perverted in reading girlie magazines. Then and after our separation I did look elsewhere.

Then Sue came on the scene for two years so I clipped my wings. When she left I was on my own and had affairs even having a go at computer dating. None of these affairs went anywhere.

Next Pam came on the scene. There was no immediate love but we were both on our own, we got on OK and our relationship developed and our two families were brought together. It went well and it seemed natural to get married and a 30 years romance followed until the big C took her. So on my own again so strayed again but not much.

A miracle happened and Sue returned into my life. Definitely an end to any thought of affairs.

Nothing much to do so I thought I would amuse myself by recounting the various ladies who have entered my life other than my wives. If you are the sensitive kind please do not read further

Names that will crop up: Beryl Davis, Janet Crane, Rowena, Pat Shadbolt,

Bernard Pendry

Zena Alford and later, Kathleen Lloyd, Anne Slade, June (stamp shop), Irene Starchy, Gillian White, Halifax audit waitress, Joan Harland IoW, Anne Camelford House and The Boardroom? Anne Marie: 4 from computer dating: Judy Marsh: Marina, Jean Graham and of course, SUE

****

The first mild stirrings was at **Beryl Davis's** 12th birthday party. Mr. & Mrs. Davis had laid on lemonade and cakes and there were about 12 of us youngsters present all excited to play the games, pass the parcel, musical chairs etc. Then Mrs. Davis said we would play postman's knock. This entailed one of us having to go out into the hallway, shout out a number and the boy or girl had to join them in the hallway, don't know what we were expected to do but when my number was called it was **Janet Crane** there. Now Janet lived just down the road from me and was a bit of a Tomboy. We looked at each other not knowing what to do but we just grinned and had a cuddle. Felt good but that was it. (Some 40 years later I walked into Boots in Oxford Street and was amazed that I recognised Janet behind the perfume counter more surprisingly she recognised me).

My dad was a member of an organisation called The Association of Supervising Electrical Engineers and was responsible for organising their annual dinner dance and even as a 12 years old got dragged along. These were definitely not for the young but another youngster in the same predicament was **Rowena** just a year older than me. We got chatting, had a few dances and even then I knew she had a very good figure. The evening ended and we parted. A couple of years later I accompanied Mum and Dad to their friend's pub just south of Bath and would you believe it; Rowena was there with her parents. One night I had gone to bed when this lovely girl came in and cuddled up. My heart raced, I knew it felt good but not knowing what to do we just chatted, end of story.

Visits to the cinema were regular trips with my mates. One night just Mick and I went to The Red Hall in Walham Green (now Fulham Broadway), hardly anyone there but a few rows in front of us were two girls so we decided to sit one each side of them. They were friendly so we fancied our chances. When the programme was over and the lights come on we stood up and the girl next to me just kept going, must have been at least 6 ft. 6. I did the decent thing and walked her home but that was it.

Age 14 the family upped and moved to The Six Bells Pub in Colerne, Wiltshire (see chapter 6) and whilst I got on well with the local boys the local girls found me an interesting object from the great city. One night **Zena Alford,** a well-proportioned girl about my age, asked me to go for a walk so hand in hand we wandered down a lane away from the village. It was pitch dark but Zena must have had cat's eyes as she lead me down the lane ending in the middle of a field. It must have been warm as we lay down on the grass and she started kissing me and was getting amorous. Soon a few clothes were coming off and before I really knew what was happening I had lost my cherry, I was flummoxed, is this what sex is supposed to be like, lasting only two or three minutes, not very exciting but now I knew how lovely a woman's body felt, so smooth like silk.

On another occasion I was necking with **Geraldine**, another shapely girl 2 years older in a quiet corner of the Village when I thought it would be nice to caress her and stroke her bare skin. She was wearing a blouse and skirt so I slipped my hand under her blouse to find she was wearing a vest. No problem, I'll just ease it up. I kept pulling but there seemed to be yards of it when she whispered, "I'm wearing a full-length slip"" I gave up content with just a kiss.

Pat Shadbolt, my age, really took a shine to me and we spent hours together and although there was no sex, she was my girlfriend. When the family moved back to Ringmer Avenue she wrote to me and sent some glamour photos of herself and for many months we corresponded. Then she said she was coming to London with her family and could we meet. Of course. We met at home and it was obvious that she was willing to make love but where could one go in those prim and proper days? Not like now when parents seem to think it best to let their children cuddle up with suitors in comfortable surroundings, Oh! that I had been so lucky. Anyway we went walking and ended up on a secluded place on the Putney side of the Thames and it was there that I had my one and only knee trembler, f…ing ridiculous, not recommended. I do think that had we stayed at Colerne, Pat and I would have married.

I had failed the 11+ thus going to the down market Fulham Central. At 13 I got a chance to change schools, passed the exam and transferred to Balham & Tooting College of Commerce (grand sounding but academically poor and sports were almost non existent). The first day there was quite traumatic. I had only ever been to all boys" schools and there were masses of girls in the playground. In the Assembly Hall we were greeted and allocated to the various classes. These turned out to be 10 boys and 30 girls. I was horrified and getting home vowed to my Mum that I had to leave. With encouragement from her I gave it a chance and soon realised that girls have other attributes than being able to play football. The most gorgeous girl in the school was **Kathleen Lloyd**, 5 feet 2 eyes of blue itchy itchy coo. We became an item but I put her on such a high pedestal that I never went further than heavy petting. This lasted all our school years and I even got dragged in to socialise with the heavy mob she associated with around Clapham Common and Balham High Road including Alfie Flowers. We exchanged letters but that was it.

Many, many years passed when I made a business phone call to a solicitor in a firm in Crawley. The telephonist asked who was calling to which I naturally replied, Bernard Pendry. There was a pause then she enquired if I had gone to BTCC. Yes it was she, so I enquired how she was and whether she had married that Alfie Flowers. Yes but not happy. Chat, chat and I asked if we could meet. She replied "tricky but possible next Tuesday as he plays darts". So it was arranged and my heart started pounding and this vision of loveliness swam before me. The days past and my excitement mounted. On the Monday she phoned and it went something like this "Bernard I was so looking forward to meeting but we had better postpone it because tomorrow I have to go into hospital and have all my teeth out". I promised to get in touch later but my ardour was well and truly crushed so that was the end of that. Maybe she would have been a fat old bird, which would have shattered my illusions, better to keep those lovely memories.

Back at school there were lots of girls to chat to. One of Kathleen's close friends was **Irene Starchy;** the best-endowed girl in the school and my mates egged me on to measure the size of her bust. She didn't object so round the back of the cycle shed I produced the tape measure, a marvelous 42 inches although this was outside her blouse. Pity.

In those days I cycled all over the place to visit some of the girls, one in particular was **Gillian White** who lived in Tottenham some 22 miles from Fulham but it was worth it as Gillian was a very loving person. Again where did one go to make love? Once we made whoopee on a gravestone, bloody cold. Wish there had been an alternative.

Other girls at school who resisted all my attempts to get closer were Barbara Goodman, who went on to marry Dennis Godwin, partner of Bob Monkhouse. She was one of the best-looking girls who stayed on for 6th form. Her best friend, Jacqueline Harding, married Bob Monkhouse. I fancied Olga Povey but she only had eyes for Ron Cunningham the best athlete in the school. I did enjoy a night with June Wells who later worked at Stanley Gibbons stamp shop in The Strand. Every time I pass a stamp shop I think of her.

My first away audit was in Halifax staying at some 3 star hotel where there was a lovely waitress named **Jeanie** who was the only other youngster in the place so we got on well and there was an immediate attraction. A few nights later she asked if I wanted to go for a walk, of course. She knew her way around and led me in the dark to a shelter in the local park. We started kissing and cuddling and things were going well with high expectations, I think for both of us, when we were caught in a flashlight pointed directly at us. Well you can imagine our reaction, was this some robber, gang member etc. "Sorry to disturb you sir, but there was a snooper round the back spying on you, so I chased him away so do carry on". It was a local bobby but as you can imagine our ardour was cooled irrevocably.

Now I was qualified, left the profession and working for a family property company who had built Tintagel House and Camelford House in Lambeth, very wealthy? Our offices were on the 17th floor (the top) and they had a luxury flat on the 16th floor, the likes of which I had never seen, quite opulent. Both had huge picture windows overlooking the Thames. The floors below were rented to The Post Office who had a canteen on the 12th floor where occasionally I would have lunch. While there I started playing bridge and the two experts were Jerry and **Anne** who taught me so much but it was Anne who attracted me in other ways.

It wasn't long before I invited her to see the offices and things just started to happen, she was even keener than I was. What a kisser and had no hesitation to stripping off to reveal the largest breasts I had seen. Once when driving through Epsom she stripped off giving passing lorry drivers an eye full. As the owners lived in Brighton I was the key holder for their flat on the 16th floor and the guest bedroom with huge mirrors was a perfect place to have fun. She taught me things I hadn't even read about. She was happily married so there was no danger of romance entanglement just occasional fun times. When I left this company to become a partner in a chartered accountants practice, these occasional meetings continued and the long couch in my office was perfect for our get togethers. After such a night our cleaner, Ron, a great chap who had been with the practice for years, pointed at a powder mark on the couch and said "that looks like a well powdered arse".

The boardroom at Camelford House had a very expensive table around which 16 board members could sit in comfort. At a Post Office Christmas party I got chatting to a bubbly, tubby girl who wanted to see my office, I thought she had certain intensions in mind and was not wrong. We toured the offices ending in the boardroom where we disrobed and made love. Nothing strange in that but then to my amazement, naked she did cartwheels all around the table. Never did see her again but the image of her always occurred at board meetings, if only the directors knew what I was thinking!

In chapter 22 you will read about my friendship with Joe Cocker how I accompanied him on a tour of The States. I had only read about groupies who followed rock stars but now saw that the stories were true not that I, or Joe for that matter, made any attempts. However, I shall always remember the Dallas gig or more to the point what happened after. The gig went like clockwork and limos were waiting outside to run us back to the hotel. I was in one waiting for anyone else when the promoter came over for a chat and asked, with a nod and a wink, if I would like to give this young lady a lift to town. Of course, so this sweet young thing got into the limo and off we went back to the hotel for a drink. After we had chatted to Joe and some of the crew I thought she would ask for a taxi but instead she asked if she could stay the night. Well why not! She certainly surprised me, after kissing and cuddling she suggested we showered together, what a firm young body, followed by a passionate night of love making (well maybe a hour!). As I lay drifting off to sleep, out of the blue she said, "Do you know how old I am?" "No and it doesn't matter" me thinking there was no problem. "Fifteen" she said. I sat bolt up right, I did know that under 16 it is statutory rape in Texas but it had not dawned on me she could be this young. She didn't seem to be making a point but from then on I had a most fretful night with nightmares as I could imagine her parents calling the police and them somehow tracing her to my room. At 6 a.m. I couldn't stand it any more so phoned Gerry Lockran, he was the solo singer/guitarist who opened each gig and who I got on well with, explained the situation and within minutes he had arrived and whisked her away. No doubt a good move for all three of us.

The tour ended with a gig in Hawaii and we stayed at the five stars Surf Rider Hotel on Waikiki Beach and one other pleasant interlude was a night of passion with a most intriguing lady from LA. She was very experienced, took a mattress out on to the moon lit balcony were we made mad passionate love overlooking the bay with the moon shining on the ocean. After, she brought out hot towels and rubbed me down. I did suggest we meet up when I returned to L.A. but she said that was not a good idea as her boyfriend was a weight lifter who had jealous tendencies. Oh! Happy days.

I was a member of Leatherhead Golf Club and one Saturday a group of us were chatting after golf when Margaret Nunn the lady secretary suggested we should go out for dinner. Various venues were suggested when someone said "How about The Cock at Headley" to which another lady shouted, "Oh I love The Cock'" to much mirth. So it was to The Cock we went. One of the party was Brenda, a fairly trim figure who unfortunately had a limp otherwise reasonably attractive. At this time I was on my own so when she suggested we go back to her place, no problem. After another drink we ended up in bed. She was so amorous but when I found she had hairy nipples, it was a right turn off, so the lovemaking went on for ages with me counting the cracks in the ceiling and her saying how fantastic I was.

After about 17 years of marriage Sheila went cold and it was not a happy situation so I was prone to straying. Anne Marie was a very attractive blonde who was a senior in the office and we got on well. Therefore it was a logical step that we started dating and lovemaking followed. She was such an exciting lady, loved being tied up and it was just an enjoyable time. However guilt came over me and I called a halt as I was determined to make another go at wooing Sheila. Some months passed and things didn't improve so I thought I would restart the affair with Anne Marie only to learn that she had now started going out with Gordon Silver one of the managers. They ended up marrying.

Now on my own what could I do for female company? Had a go at DATELINE what is now computer dating. First date was with **Sheila** from Horsham, pleasant 44 years old nurse who was recently divorced and it soon became clear all she was seeking was a replacement to give her security. All I was looking for was a bit of fun and gave her advice "If you thought a guy was worth considering you should have sex even on the first night because if the sex was good a relationship may follow not the other way round". "No no couldn't dream of that" so after a goodnight kiss, we parted. Couple of days later I received a phone call from her saying "I've thought about your advice and would like to give it a try so why don't you come and stay the night?" I replied "Sheila a lovely thought but the moment has past".

The only one from Dateline that I had a fling with was **Jennifer** from Orpington that lasted from early December 1982 until 8th January. During this time she stayed over with me on many occasions and I thought we were getting on well. Then all of a sudden she was gone, disappeared and I couldn't contact her again. Could it have been my lack of charm, surely not, must have been the journey from Orpington!

My last attempt at Dateline was with **Hazel,** 29, good looking, works for The Ministry of Defense, so what could go wrong? After many drink she was so opinionated and thought she was always right, I wonder who she reminded me of! It's opposites that attract.

About this time neighbour **Judy Marsh** and I got on very well although she was rather neurotic and never seemed at ease but it was fun while it lasted.

I had a strange phone conversation similar to the one with Kathleen Lloyd when I phoned a solicitor in Sutton and the telephonist asked the same question, did I go to BTCC? To my "yes" answer she said she was **Anne Slade** who was in my class and later went on the school trip to Belgium with the school. She lived in Stockwell, divorced and had a grown up son living with her. So it was obvious we must meet up and an affair followed but like with Jennifer it was always her visiting me. It was the same result, after a couple of months she disappeared and I never found out why or how to contact her. My magnetic charm must be working in reverse!

I was a member of The Wimbledon Squash & Badminton Club and one of my friends was Dave Timperley, a very strange character married to a Swedish sexy lady, **Marina**. They had a strange relationship and you never knew whether they were together or apart. One evening at the Club he announced that the previous night when he got home the front door was locked but he could hear some noise so he looked through the letterbox to see a man's bare arse fleeing down the hall presumably out the back door to safety. He was convinced that it was one of us and said he could recognise the arse so he had us all dropping our trousers. We all got a clean bill of health. It was years later, after they separated that Marina and I did have a one off session.

One of my out of town clients was the farmer family Miles. Jim had divorced his wife, **April**, and set up with a much younger lady. April phoned me and asked if I would accompany her to the Hunt Ball, as she needed a partner. Never been to a Hunt Ball so seemed a good idea especially when she said I could stay the night saving me from a long journey home from Heathfield. What a splendid affair, good food, lots of square dancing, taught her to jive and lots of interesting chatting. The drive home was something different with me driving and when we got to her place she was just wild and a great time was had. She wanted to start a relationship but for me this was a one off.

APPENDIX 8

TIT BITS

MY FIRST CURRY

Growing up in Fulham Mum had never heard of curry so I had no idea what it tasted like a group of us went to Birmingham for Doug's marriage to Anne. On the eve we went to an Indian Restaurant and I just asked them to order me something. Well I certainly was unprepared; it was so hot I thought my mouth was on fire and even with a glass of water with each mouthful it didn't help. After sweating I did manage to eat half of it. Over the years it did not improve so I am limited to Korma.

THE GARDEN ROLLER

When we moved into 30 Ruxley Lane there was an ancient garden roller in a hedge near the house and there it lay for many years. Pam said it would be nice if I could move it to the end of the garden. So I dragged it onto the lawn and started to push and got up a bit of speed. The roller was in 2 halves and going at full speed towards the walnut tree I changed direction. The 2 halves locked and I flew over the handle bar giving an impression of Superman landing in a heap. Pam didn't know whether to laugh or rush to my help. Laughing took priority.

TUFTY

Daughter Nicola age about 14 said she had a secret to tell me and hoped I wouldn't be cross. She had been spending most of her spare time at Keith Tollick's stables, mainly as she put it, shovelling horseshit. But her favourite horse was Tufty and for some reason they had to get rid of it. To save this she had taken £500 out of her Post Office book and bought it. I told her I was so proud of her for taking the initiative and gave her a cuddle.

The next time Nicola wanted a chat was many years later. She had been cohabiting with Steve for a year or two and they had bought a flat in Surbiton. But the magic had gone and she wanted out although didn't want to hurt Steve. My advice was that when love had gone there was no easy way to end a relationship and a swift break was less painful in the long run. So taking my advice we drove to the flat she packed a bag and moved back to Ruxley Lane. The heartache on both sides was soon over.

THE WHISTLE

Brother Reg had this very loud whistle without using any fingers and with some practice taught me how to do it. It has stood me in good stead throughout my life, rounding up the kids, getting attention whenever etc. As much as I have tried I have never been successful in teaching anyone. In the years between Pam and Sue I joined the Epsom Male Voice Choir thinking it would be fun to have a singsong however it was nothing like I had envisaged. They certainly were an enjoyable bunch and did their best to encourage me but it was hopeless, they had all been choristers and I was like a fish out of water. However, they were practicing First World War songs for a performance at Epsom Playhouse. Now one of the songs related the soldiers being pinned down in the trenches with Jerry bombs whizzing down to which they went "weeeeeee boom." I thought it would be fun to use my loud whistle imitating the sound a falling bomb would make. Well the choir master immediately said your in, that whistle would be great. Sad to say I chickened out.

THE ROLEX WATCH

On holiday in Spain with Sheila and Ginge I was accosted by a looky/looky man trying to sell me a "Genuine Rolex watch" for say, 100 pesetas.

Bernard Pendry

Now remember this was my first trip to such an exotic place so when he kept knocking the price down reaching 20 pesetas, I had to buy. But how to get it back through customs? Ginge and I discussed the situation and like a true friend he agreed to smuggle it back in the bottom of his binocular case. What a relief when we got through. At this stage I was working for the Hunnisett's and in their group they owned two jewellers shops and at the one just off Trafalgar Square a watch repairer was employed. So on the Monday of my return I proudly took my *Rolex*" expecting him to congratulate me on such a fantastic buy. I was quite shocked when he told me it certainly was not a Rolex but was about the same as a Timex most likely to have been made in Ireland. Crestfallen but what a good lesson in life!

A NICE POLICEMAN

My close mate Alan Dodsworth a.k.a. Babe was the 4th son of a motor cycling family and during his life had many motorbikes. Triumph Trophy, Manx Norton, Velocette, Harley Davidsons to name but a few. He bought a converted bike, part Triumph part Norton made for racing and it was fast. One very early morning in about 1954 he was heading west approaching the Kingston-by-pass, when he was pulled over by a traffic cop on his Triumph. The conversation went something like this Babe "what's the problem?" Cop "none I am just fascinated by your bike. What speed can it do?" Alan "never had it full out, but it is quick" Cop "there is no traffic about so how about a race?" Babe "you sure?" Cop "yes let's go". So they haired off reaching speeds of over a hundred. I think the outcome was a tie after 5 miles.

A SHOULDER RUB

Back in the 70/80s on a Friday night after squash it was over to 'Argy's' the local Indian restaurant before back to my place for cards, normally 3-card brag. On this occasion Terry Morgan, Keith's wife was watching and when John Harris complained of a stiff shoulder she started to massage them when there was a power cut and the lights went out. She continued massaging when Roy Oldaker gently knocked her aside and took over the massaging. Being a past speedway rider his grip was something to behold and the massaging got more severe. John "Oo! Terry not so hard, Terry it really hurts, Terry stop". The lights came back on to great mirth.

GARDEN PARTY

All the family including aunt, uncle and cousins came, fun, food, games and lots of singing the old songs. In the garden was a pond that was covered by substantial netting to protect against herons. Aunty Pam was a little tipsy and somehow fell into the pond rolling about on the netting showing off her large bloomers. I had to stop brother Reg from treading on the netting otherwise it would have collapsed and they would sink but he did manage to pull her out. The story went round that Pam had fallen in the pond and everyone thought that it was my Pam. Husband Len was not amused.

COOL HAND LUKE

I think I am the only person who thought the film stupid firstly because he found himself in a chain gang for the crime of cutting the heads off parking meters. Then trying to break a record for eating hard-boiled eggs and being a total idiot with the way he carried on, ending up dead. Another was *The Day of the Jackal*" when the baddies hired the top assassin in the world to kill President De Gaulle. Throughout the film his preparations went on and on until the time came, De Gaulle was making a speech, he was hidden on the top of a nearby building long range rifle with De Gaulle in his sights, finger ready to pull the trigger, which he did as De Gaulle bent down to pick something up, film over. It was like a Tom & Jerry ending.

TRACY AND THE BUSINESS

Tracy came into my life when I got together with her mum, Pam; she was a working housewife being a cook at various institutions. She had had problems with credit cards of which she had a few and was in problems. We had a chat, I loaned her sufficient funds to clear all debts on the promise she would not use them again. All went well no problem.

I got a call one day from her that she would like to come and discuss a project. There was an empty shop unit in Ruxley Lane that she thought would be a good location for her to open a restaurant/café but had no idea of how to go about it. Lots of discussions with her and husband Pete followed, the result being she took a lease of the property, with limited funds and a small loan from me she equipped the place out with a variety of furniture including church pews for seating, cutlery from the Internet, after lots of ideas named the place THE BUSINESS, employed her friend Sue and opened on 12th September 2001. I insisted on being the first customer so was there just before 7.30 and the two ladies were behind the counter expectantly. In came a group of workmen, they froze like rabbits caught in the head lights, it was Ray Trafford a local fencer (no, not with a epee) with his workers, "Bligh-me boys look they have the Daily Mail, next they will have the Times". With that he ordered a full breakfast for them all and he did this every workday only interrupted when he spent a spell as a guest of Her Majesty.

I had many breakfasts at The Business, my favourite being a pair of kippers for only £1.50. Later I told Tracy she should increase the price, which she did to £2.00, then told me I was the only one who ate them.

FISHY WATER

  In the hall at Ruxley Lane there was a large fish tank sitting on a cupboard that housed the filtration system. There were just two large fish one looking like a monster that attacked whenever you pressed your face to the glass. Anyway we were going away for the weekend and asked the neighbours to feed them once a day. Opening the front door when we returned home it was splosh the place was flooded, the tank almost empty with the two fish swimming on their sides. The neighbour's assured us that everything was OK when they fed them yesterday but what had happened was the filtration system had continued pumping the water out but the return system had failed. Saved the fish, sorted out the system then the insurance claim.

The insurance assessor was a charming man and his first impression was that the carpet could be dried. It took a bit of persuading but he did agree that drying might not be the answer and put through a claim for the whole of the carpet, that included not only the hall but also the staircase and the L shaped landing. Some thought that I had bribed him but he was just a nice fellow.

SOD THE INSTITUTE OF CHARTERED ACCOUNTANTS

1990 I had retired and we went away on holiday for 4 weeks. When I returned home there was a letter from The Institute informing me that my fees were overdue. The upshot was they expected me to reapply for membership with a reference and £160. This after 31 years as a member. Of course I made a fuss but they were intransigent so "up theirs" and I was no longer entitled to put FCA behind my name. So what, I never intended to practice again.

CAMDEN LOCK

One December day in 1979 we all (Sheila, Mark and me) went to Camden Lock to see KOKOMO a group that included Neil Hubbard and Alan Spenner who I acted for and had been part of The Grease Band, backers of Joe Cocker. Great gig then a hubbub went round "have you seen the weather?" When the gig ended out we went to find 12 inches of snow. Slipping and sliding I managed to get the car to a main road and slithered as far as Fulham when I decided it was too dangerous to continue so called into Mum & Dad's. It was now 2 a.m. but they welcomed us with open arms and we bedded down for the night. Aren't parents lovely!

APPENDIX 9

OTHER THINGS

DANCING

Age 16 I attended Leweline's Dance Studio in Clapham Junction for regular lessons and after a fashion mastered the Waltz, Quickstep and a basic Foxtrot but nothing further. These lessons stood me in good stead throughout my life, just wish I had mastered the Tango.

When Babe and I were 17 we went to Eel Pie Island a famous jive island in the Thames. Now there is a bridge but in those days you had to get rowed over. Great music and the first place I learnt to jive which became my favourite dance and I really fancied myself as pretty good.

Age about 18 my parents took in lodgers one of whom was an attractive German young lady who liked ballroom dancing. So I invited her to the Lyceum Ballroom in London and we had a great time. What fascinated me was going one way I glided around but the other way was a struggle. I found out later the place used to be a cinema and the floor sloped. Many years later it was leveled.

Unfortunately, ballroom and jive took up too much space so many venues went over to disco and silly dances like The Creep where couples basically stayed on one spot, and then there was The Mashed Potato, The Bump and others that escape me.

While staying with Curtis & Glenda in Texas Pam & I were invited to a couples 60th wedding anniversary some hours drive away. Being in Texas we thought it would be country & western music but no, it was a German Oompha band. Unfortunately, we had let Curtis know that we were keen jivers so were horrified when he let the band know and requested them to play a jive especially for us. It is hard to imagine a German Oompha band playing a jive but they made an attempt so what could we do but give it a go. It was awful but we got a great applause.

I always fancied myself as a raunchy jiver and could go on for ages. That is until a group holiday at the Burstin Hotel in Folkstone with a dance floor in the basement. After a few jives I partnered June Conboy and had to quit after about 30 minutes. She went on all evening without a brake.

Over the years I taught Pam, Sue, Nicola and Nikki to jive and earlier jived threesomes with Sheila & Pam.

One of the most enjoyable dances was a Masked Ball at The Royal Automobile Club when I took the whole family, Steph & Mark, Nikki & Mike, Nicola & Neil, Tracy & Pete and Jenny & Dave. It was great watching the couples, no ballroom but lots of Disco music

RATIONING

I don't know whether toilet rolls were rationed but we had newspaper squares in the toilets and if lucky phone books torn in half. The thought of it now is quite unimaginable.

MUM'S PEARLS OF WISDOM

Things that Mum taught me that last a lifetime.

When peeing into a toilet aim for the porcelain not directly into the water. This she learnt from an Irish lodger who always urinated straight into the water making quite a noise.

Another toilet hint was never immediately follow someone into the loo! Could be embarrassing.

If you have nothing good to say, say nothing. Oh how I wish I could have lived by this!

SO CALLED FRIENDS

KEITH MORGAN AND BARRY (BADGER) STILL friends from the Squash club days. Independently I had acted as their accountant but they moved on and surprised everyone when they went into business together running the Mad Hatter Pub. I had little contact with them until I got a phone call from Keith "Can we come and see you as we have a problem" At the ensuing meeting Keith said they had a cash flow problem, they owed £3,500 to a supplier who refused to deliver any more goods and a big weekend trade was looming. So I asked what they wanted me to do? It was obvious they wanted me to loan them some money so I asked, "If I paid the supplier how long would it be to get repaid". Like in chorus both said, "After this good weekend it should be within a week". Much against my better judgment I paid the supplier.

Months went by, they fell out, parted company with Badger staying at The Mad Hatter and Keith taking over The Castle Pub. When asking Keith when I would be paid he said that in their split agreement it was down to Badger.

After many requests Badger did pay me £500 but it was always "don't worry Bernst (sic) you will get paid". After this went on for some time I instructed my solicitor to issue a writ. He said "Do you realize you already have a judgment summons against Mr. Still for £900 unpaid accountancy fees. Shall I add that to the writ?" Why not indeed. Then he enquired whether he should attach the claim to the house for security. So yes. The issuing of the writs had no effect so we went to court, Keith turned up but no Badger. Keith pleaded that Badger owed the debt, as that was part of their agreement. The judge said "Mr. Morgan whatever your arrangement with your ex partner has no bearing whatsoever on your liability to Mr. Pendry". A judgment summons was issued in my favour including my costs but with time to pay as agreed by me.

Badger was in the process of some scam to sell his house to his mother and got a shock when my entire claim had to be paid before the sale could be completed.

The result being I got all my money and costs but lost two old friends. Should have stood by the old saying *never a borrower or lender be.*

BARRY CLAYTON "WIMBLE" and Pub Golf. He had the idea for getting pubs to form golf teams and then arranging golf days for them in competitive tournaments. The idea interested me as it could be aligned to GCGB so we entered into an agreement, I would let him use one of my offices rent free, prepare the necessary documentation for no costs, he would promote the idea to various pubs and if any profit arose we would split it 50/50. All went well until he got the Publican Magazine interested in promoting the idea then without any discussion he said our agreement was ended. Of course I protested and had a chat with my solicitor who after hearing the story advised that although I had a good case but knowing the person and his finances advised against instigating a court case. So I let the matter drop. You only hear from Wimble when he wants something, as many friends will contest.

THE GALLEON

Good friend Nick Preece and wife Sally had just moved into the huge house in Walton on the Hill and were seeking things to fill the house. I went with him to an auction house in Westerham, Kent, as there were items of furniture that he had picked out. Wandering round the auction room he paid some attention to a fine 4-mast galleon but showed no real interest.

When the auction started we were sitting together and he bid for various items of furniture with some success. Up came the galleon and the bidding started. I thought it would be a nice new house present so I entered the bidding. Up it went, through the twenties, through the thirties and forties into the fifties, when the auctioneer said, "are you two gentlemen together only you are bidding against each other". What embarrassment, however he still has it sitting in the entrance hall.

Bernard Pendry

APPENDIX 10

OTHER GOLF STORIES

DAD & RAY SAUNDERS

Dad's frequent partner in the 1960s was Ray Saunders who would turn up at Ringmer about 6 a.m. on a Saturday morning the door to be opened by Dad in his pyjamas saying "I'll just take a cuppa up to Al, I'll be down soon but make yourself one". Then off they would go for a round of golf in all kinds of weather.

ARMY BARRACKS

Ray Saunders arranged for Keith Drayton, Archie and I to join him on a golfing trip to Kent to play Royal St Georges G.C., Walmer & Kingsdown G.C. and one other. At the time Ray was in the Met Police and knew they had a tie-up with the army so arranged for us to be billeted at their Manston Barracks in the Warrant Officers quarters, for a shilling or two. On checking in and reporting to the sergeant in charge, Ray explained we were police and had been invited to stay. The sergeant took one look at Archie, all 5 feet 2 of him, and said "He is no policeman". Ray quick as a flash said "No he is in the vehicle repair department". A great long weekend followed.

GCGB TRIP TO FLORIDA

The trip to Sanibel Island had been arranged for 31 of us. An odd number so it was arranged that I would share with Brian Jackson and Kate, the organizer would have a room to herself. The party were to arrive on the

Wednesday but I was in Miami so set off on Tuesday across Alligator Alley, 125 miles of dead straight road, and arrived at the resort about 11.00 p.m. On checking into our room I discovered that the single bed, a huge double king size was in the premier room overlooking the golf course whereas the double bedroom was small and had hardly any view. Being the founder of the GCGB I considered this unfair so set about getting the beds changed. First I was going to get the giant bed out of the room intending it for the small room. Even Sampson would have had difficulties and after about an hour of struggle all I managed to do was get the mattress wedged in the doorway. No option but to explain the problem to reception. "No problem sir, we will have it fixed by morning". Managed to get it back and went to sleep. As it turned out Brian never slept in a bed just using the adequate sofa, so Kate had the small double room.

DON'T LOOSE AT SPOOF

On another trip to Florida, this time with Nick Preece to buy ourselves new sets of golf clubs, we were booked into a two-bedroom apartment. Same again, one room had a sauna, huge lounge and balcony over looking the golf course. The other was small and just had the lift shaft for a view. Who was to have the choice? We decided to spoof (a chance game known to gamblers) best of 5. I went 2 up then lost the next 3. Nick was generous and occasionally let me stay on his balcony!

Still on Spoof eight of us from Wimbledon Squash Club went to West Byfleet Squash Club to support our team. In the bar afterwards we played spoof for who was to buy the drinks. Three of the group had never played before and as I was a grand master there was no doubt I would not be buying. Well something went wrong, I lost, then I lost, then I lost, then I lost, then I lost five on the trot, quite costly. We then went to a local restaurant and it was suggested we spoof for who pays, guess what my answer was?

Bernard Pendry

THE GOLF HAT

With the GCGB we were playing on a course near Brighton, Sussex. Sally Preece was in my fourball and before we teed off she had to go into the pro shop to buy a hat. She returned hatless, her reason being the name of the course was **THE DYKE**.

BEST TO KNOW THE RULES

Mid Surrey Squash Club were playing Fraser Court Squash Club a challenge match at Hever Castle G.C. Ray was playing Nick Preece and on one hole Nick hit his approach shot well through the green and up a steep bank at the back. His ball lodged against a tree. He then said to Ray "as it is against a tree I get a free drop" (understand that at this stage neither of them had much idea about the rules) and with this he dropped his ball clear. It rolled down the hill, bumpety bump and ended on the green. Ray protested but to no avail. It took years for Ray to get over this once he learnt the rules.

This time in a friendly challenge Ray was playing Roy Roper, a golf novice. On one hole, from just off the edge of the green, Roy chipped and his ball lodged against the flagstick. Ray briskly walked over, grabbed the flagstick and sent Roy's ball flying. When Roy protested Ray said "haven't you heard of a stymie? If the opponent gets to the hole first he has the right to eject the ball?" and Roy fell for it. (A stymie disappeared years ago. It was if the player's opponent's ball was between his ball and the hole, he was stymied and therefore he had no option other than to putt around it or try a jump shot). Anyway a few holes later Roy hit another good chip that looked as though it was heading for the cup so without hesitation he ran after it just in case.

LOST BALL

Coming down the 16th on The Princes Course one day Dad had driven off to the left leaving him to negotiate a sturdy oak. For once he made good contact and the ball flew at the oak. Now people tell you that a tree is 90% air but his ball decided this was not true and it lodged in a forked branch some 15 feet high. Rescue was out of the question and I wonder whether it is still there to this day!

PUTNEY PARK GOLF SOCIETY

What wonderful memories this stirs. The Society played on the municipal courses in Richmond Park, my first game being in 1948 when Dad took me for a game. Then just played intermittently with friends until I became a member of PPGS meaning you were a real golfer with a handicap and regular competitions on either the Dukes or Princes Courses. From then on it was golf every weekend.

One funny incident was on a chilly winter's morning with thick fog we were peering into the fog waiting for the agreed cry "Is it OK to drive" the cry came back "We've found our balls but can't find our clubs". Such was the enthusiasm in those days to play in all conditions even the red ball for snow.

THE JOLA CUP

Great mate Keith Drayton, also a member of PPGS, and his wife Joan spent many evenings with Sheila and I playing cards. Keith and I decided we would have an annual golf match to decide who would pay for a meal out and we bought a fine cup named The Jola Cup (guess how we thought of this name?). It was played for eleven years me edging a 6/5 winner.

LEATHERHEAD GOLF CLUB

John Upton, one of the crowd at the squash club was also a keen golfer and a member of Leatherhead Golf Club. We played a couple of games then I joined. I cannot remember if there was a waiting period which was common in those days but he was quite well in so a few doors may have been opened. In those halcyon days the M25 had not even been thought of and the old clubhouse was a cosy enjoyable place to be on a Saturday or Sunday morning, no mid week golf for me in those days as work definitely came first. I remember my first game as a member, I turned up one Saturday morning with nothing planned but an old boy by the name of Eric Parsons asked if I would make up a fourball, partnering him against two of his mates. He told me they were playing for a few bob but said I needn't get involved. Even so I felt a responsibility not to lose him money but try as I might, my game was rubbish. Coming to the eighteenth he had held them to all square then lo and behold the golfing gods favoured me, I pared and with my stroke won the hole so he picked up the money. Don't know how much but definitely out of my league. He was very grateful. After a few years John Harris another regular at Wimbledon Squash Club joined and we teamed up as a regular Saturday pairs. We did nothing spectacular but were always seen as a pair to be wary of and won more than we lost.

Of all the other memorable games that stick out in my mind was the Invitation Day sometime in the mid eighties when my guest, Ray Saunders and I played with John Harris and his guest, Dave Timperley. What a cracking game of golf it was with us all playing quality shots. Our morning fourball scores were 44 to their 42 and the afternoon greensome was our 42 to their 41. We knew these were good scores but as we were out near the front we had to wait all day to see if we had won. Ray and I took first prize and they were second so had they been playing any other pair they would have won £20 instead of handing it over to us.

GREAT EMBARRASSMENT

The nadir (lowest point) in my golfing life was in a pro/am tournament at LGC. John Harris and I were lucky enough to draw one of Britain's most prestigious golfer of all time, Neil Coles and his son playing off scratch. We were going great with both John and I doing our fair share. Neil hit every fairway, hit every green but didn't look like sinking a putt so he scored 18 pars. We came to the par 4 eighteenth with both John and I getting a shot. Four good drives, Neil and son hit the green and both got pars. John was 30 yards to the left and I was on the green some

15 feet from the pin. John hit a superb pitch and sank the putt for a 4 net 3. There was a considerable crowd around the green and the message came that we needed me to par to win the tournament. The putt was slightly down hill, I felt quite confident and struck the putt as I thought was required but it did not roll down the hill coming up 4 feet short. Not a word was said and now the enormity of the situation seized me. I tried to remain composed but felt that all eyes were on me. The putt went tantilising close but slid past on the right. The silence was palpable. So Neil did not win the £1,000 first prize, we didn't even get 2nd place or 3rd place losing on count back. Oh! How I wished I could have that putt again.

TRYING FOR A NEW CLUB

When I left Leatherhead G.C. I made enquiries of joining other clubs I went for an interview at Burhill G. C. didn't hear from them then it was Surbiton G.C. but after an interview I still didn't hear anything. When I enquired they had no recollection so a second interview. Without any explanation my application was turned down. I've wondered why but Ron the barman, ex Leatherhead barman, did warn me that they were not accepting anyone over 50 presumably because they were reaching retirement and could play too much golf.

I wasn't left pondering for long as an acceptance from the RAC arrived and I was invited to join without even an interview (they know a good thing when they see it!).

The RAC is something special and I hope to be a member forever. Best thing that happened to me was meeting Alan Borley. I had turned up for a competition and was due to play two other members who it turned out had gone off on the other course. Saying to starter Len "what happens now?" he said he would have strong words with the offenders but suggested I join a two ball due off in 5 minutes. Low and behold one of them was Alan and we have remained friends for golf but also snooker, poker and socialising.

Bernard Pendry

HOLES IN ONE

Throughout my golfing days everyone has admired my beautiful swing and are amazed that I have never been into single figures, that is until they see my pitching and chipping with which I have a constant battle. I know all the theory, have had hours of practice, lessons but still I can miss a green only 20 yards away.

I have had two holes in one, both in 1989, none before and none since. The first was at St. Mellion G. C. in Devon while playing with The Fork & Putter Golf Society as a guest of Ray Saunders. It was on the second hole, a par 3 to a slightly raised green, beautiful 6 iron, knew it was good but didn't discover it had gone in the hole until we got there. Cost me a few pounds in the bar afterwards. The next was on the 16th hole at Cuddington G. C. playing with Nick Preece, Chris Oliver & friend, big 8 iron and this time did see it go into the hole. I had a caddy so sent him ahead to order a bottle of champagne.

Nick never got a hole in one but playing Hankley Common G. C. on the long par 3 tenth his tee shot swerved off into thick gorse. His provisional shot with a 4 iron went into the hole. I said we could find his first ball but he said no way content with a 3. Wife Sally still thinks it counts as a hole in one.

Lightning Source UK Ltd.
Milton Keynes UK
UKHW022214110822
407187UK00006B/616